PB00-916201
NTSB/HAR-00/01

NATIONAL TRANSPORTATION SAFETY BOARD

WASHINGTON, D.C. 20594

HIGHWAY ACCIDENT REPORT

GREYHOUND MOTORCOACH
RUN-OFF-THE-ROAD ACCIDENT
BURNT CABINS, PENNSYLVANIA
JUNE 20, 1998

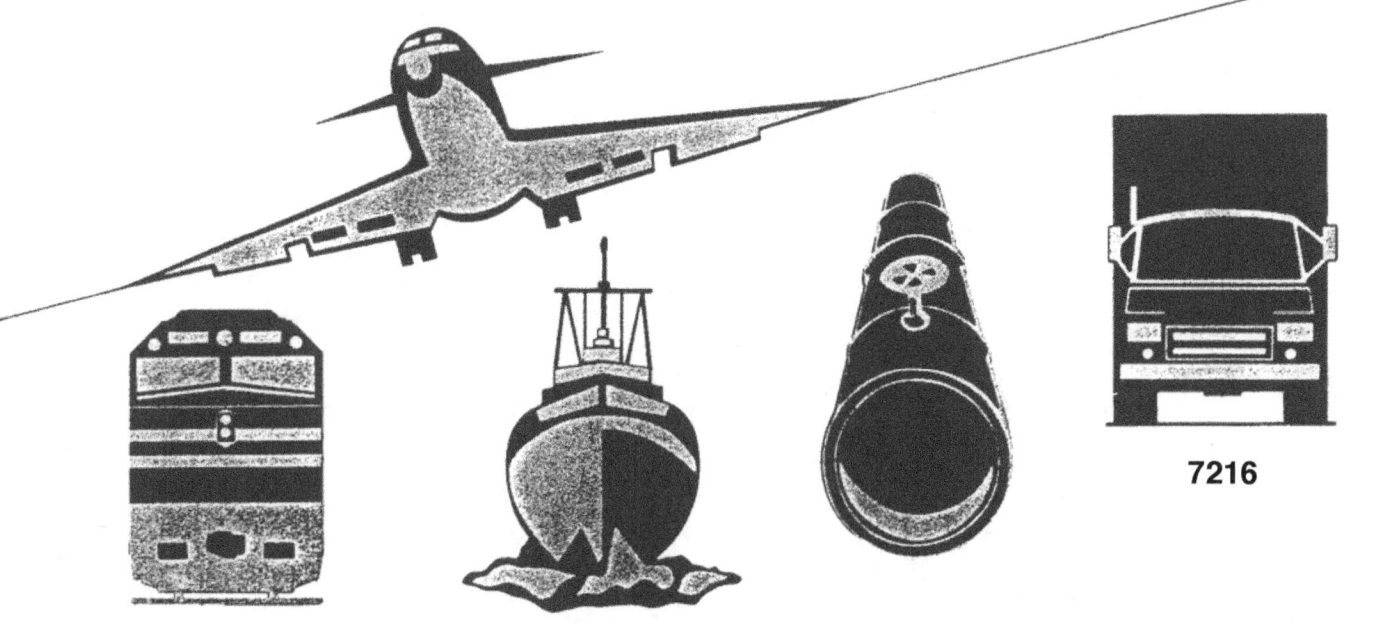

7216

National Transportation Safety Board. 2000. *Greyhound Motorcoach Run-off-the-Road Accident, Burnt Cabins, Pennsylvania, June 20, 1998.* Highway Accident Report NTSB/HAR-00/01. Washington, DC.

Abstract: On June 20, 1998, about 4:05 a.m., on the Pennsylvania Turnpike near Burnt Cabins, Pennsylvania, a Greyhound Lines, Inc., motorcoach traveled off the right side of the roadway into an emergency parking area. It struck the back of a parked tractor-semitrailer, which was pushed forward and struck the left side of another parked tractor-semitrailer. Of the 23 people on board the bus, the driver and 6 passengers were killed; the other 16 passengers were injured. The two occupants of the first tractor-semitrailer were injured, and the occupant of the second tractor-semitrailer was uninjured.

The major safety issues discussed in this report are the busdriver's performance, the adequacy of carrier oversight, the adequacy of the design and the appropriateness of the use of pull-off areas, the lack of motorcoach emergency interior lighting and retroreflective signage, and the organization of the disaster preparedness and emergency response management.

As a result of its investigation, the Safety Board issued recommendations to the National Highway Traffic Safety Administration; the Pennsylvania Turnpike Commission; Greyhound Lines, Inc.; the United Motorcoach Association; and the American Bus Association.

Highway Accident Report

Greyhound Motorcoach
Run-off-the-Road Accident
Burnt Cabins, Pennsylvania
June 20, 1998

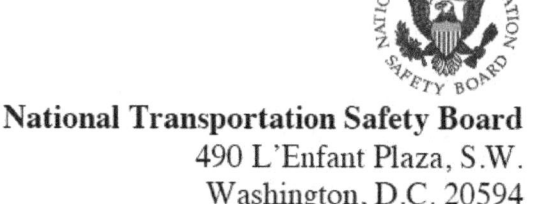

NTSB/HAR-00/01
PB00-916201
Notation 7216
Adopted: January 5, 2000

National Transportation Safety Board
490 L'Enfant Plaza, S.W.
Washington, D.C. 20594

Contents

Acronyms and Abbreviations

AASHTO	American Association of State Highway and Transportation Officials
ABA	American Bus Association
AFIP	Armed Forces Institute of Pathology
ATA	American Trucking Associations, Inc.
CAD	computer-aided dispatch
CDL	commercial drivers' license
CFR	*Code of Federal Regulations*
Commission	Pennsylvania Turnpike Commission
communications center	Operations Control Center
DDEC	Detroit Diesel Electronic Controls
Detroit Diesel	Detroit Diesel Corporation
DOT	U.S. Department of Transportation
DPS	Department of Public Safety
ECM	electronic control module
ECU	electronic control unit
EKG	electrocardiogram
EMA	Emergency Management Agency
EMS	emergency medical services
EMT	emergency medical technician
FAA	Federal Aviation Administration
FHWA	Federal Highway Administration
FMCSR	*Federal Motor Carrier Safety Regulations*
FMVSS	*Federal Motor Vehicle Safety Standards*
FSP	full-service plaza
Greyhound	Greyhound Lines, Inc.
IC	incident commander
ICS	Incident Command System
MP	milepost
MUTCD	*Manual on Uniform Traffic Control Devices*
NHTSA	National Highway Traffic Safety Administration
NMN	National Motorcoach Network
Oliver	Oliver Trucking Incorporated
OMCHS	Office of Motor Carriers and Highway Safety

PSP	Pennsylvania State Police
TEA 21	Transportation Equity Act for the 21st Century
Trailways	Trailways Incorporated
TransAm	TransAm Trucking Incorporated
TRI	Trucking Research Institute
UMA	United Motorcoach Association
VRU	voice response unit

Executive Summary

About 4:05 a.m. on June 20, 1998, a 1997 Motor Coach Industries 47-passenger motorcoach, operated by Greyhound Lines, Inc., was on a scheduled trip from New York City to Pittsburgh, Pennsylvania, traveling westbound on the Pennsylvania Turnpike near Burnt Cabins, Huntingdon County, Pennsylvania. As the bus approached milepost (MP) 184.9, it traveled off the right side of the roadway into an "emergency parking area,"[1] where it struck the back of a parked tractor-semitrailer, which was pushed forward and struck the left side of another parked tractor-semitrailer. Of the 23 people on board the bus, the driver and 6 passengers were killed; the other 16 passengers were injured. The two occupants of the first tractor-semitrailer were injured, and the occupant of the second tractor-semitrailer was uninjured.

The National Transportation Safety Board determines that the probable cause of this accident was the busdriver's reduced alertness resulting from ingesting a sedating antihistamine and from his fatigued condition resulting from Greyhound Lines, Inc., scheduling irregular work-rest periods. Contributing to the severity of the accident was the Pennsylvania Turnpike Commission's practice of routinely permitting nonemergency parking in pull-off areas within the highway clear zone.

The major safety issues identified in this accident are the busdriver's performance, the adequacy of carrier oversight, the adequacy of the design and the appropriateness of the use of pull-off areas, the lack of motorcoach emergency interior lighting and retroreflective signage, and the organization of the disaster preparedness and emergency response management.

As a result of this accident investigation, the Safety Board makes recommendations to the National Highway Traffic Safety Administration; the Pennsylvania Turnpike Commission; Greyhound Lines, Inc.; the United Motorcoach Association; and the American Bus Association.

---

[1] The 28-foot-wide 1,000-foot-long area off the roadway was used for vehicular parking.

Factual Information

Accident Narrative

Introduction

About 4:05 a.m. on June 20, 1998, a 1997 Motor Coach Industries 47-passenger motorcoach, operated by Greyhound Lines, Inc. (Greyhound), was on a scheduled trip from New York City to Pittsburgh, Pennsylvania, westbound on the Pennsylvania Turnpike near Burnt Cabins, Huntingdon County, Pennsylvania. (See figure 1.) The bus was carrying the driver and 22 passengers.

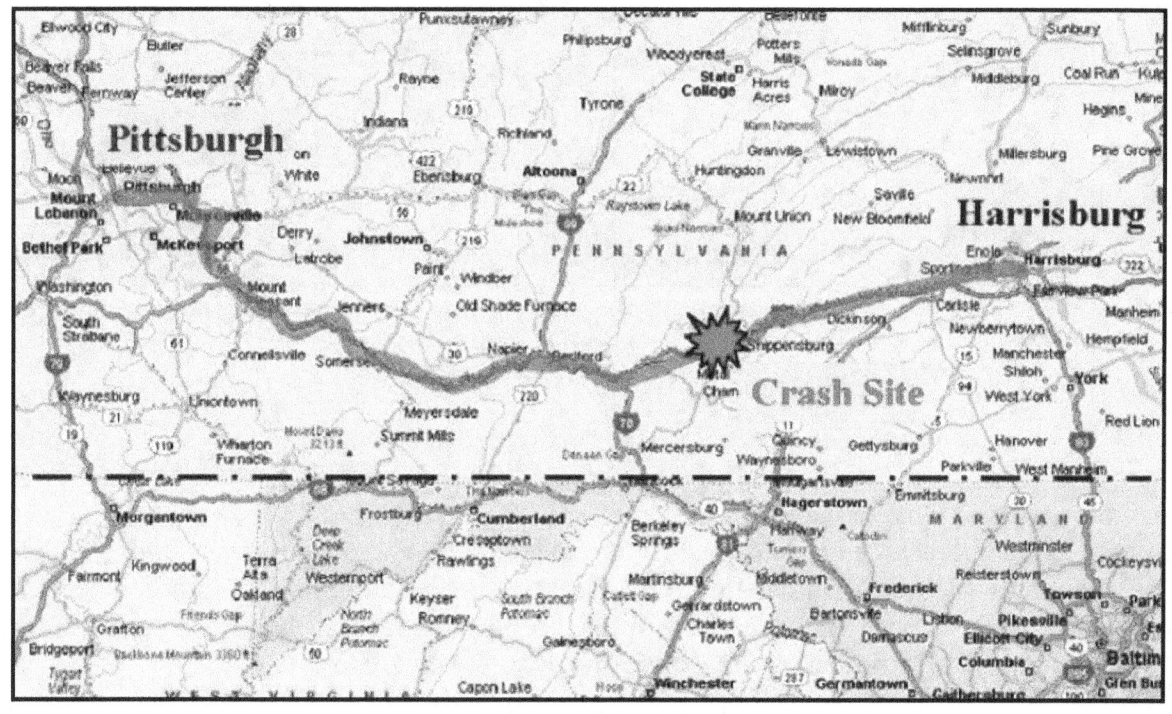

Figure 1. Map of accident area.

As the bus approached MP 184.9, it traveled off the right side of the roadway, at a departure angle of between 3 and 4 degrees, into an "emergency parking area" and struck the back of a TransAm Trucking Incorporated (TransAm) parked tractor-semitrailer, which was pushed forward and struck the left side of an Oliver Trucking Incorporated (Oliver) tractor-semitrailer, parked in front of the TransAm vehicle. (See appendix B for information on the TransAm and Oliver vehicles.)

According to the TransAm truckdriver, he and his codriver were sleeping in their truck's sleeper berth at the time of the accident. About 1:30 a.m., he had stopped his vehicle, leaving its parking lights on, in the parking area, about 9 to 10 feet from the edge of the travel lane, because it was raining heavily at that time.[1] They were awakened and injured by the severity of the impact. The Oliver truckdriver was also sleeping in his truck's sleeper berth at the time of the collision. The TransAm truckdriver said that the area[2] was a common place for truckdrivers to stop and rest and that he noticed about four other trucks parked there. (See figure 2.) (See appendix B for information on the occupants of the TransAm and Oliver trucks.)

Figure 2. View of accident.

About 5 minutes after the accident occurred, another Greyhound bus was on the turnpike en route to Breezewood, Pennsylvania, when the driver saw the accident bus, which appeared to be parked with its lights off, on the shoulder area.[3] The busdriver said that he observed that the bus had crashed into the rear of a tractor-semitrailer and he pulled off the road to help. He pounded on the door of a tractor-semitrailer behind the accident bus and asked the occupant to call 911 on her cellular phone; he then used her phone to call the Greyhound maintenance response division in Dallas, Texas.

Of the 23 people on board the bus, the driver and 6 passengers were killed; the other 16 passengers sustained serious to minor injuries. The two occupants of the TransAm tractor-semitrailer received serious and minor injuries, and the occupant of the Oliver tractor-semitrailer was uninjured.

---

[1] Accu-Weather Forecasts for the Pennsylvania Turnpike stated that a cluster of showers and thunderstorms, moving slowly southward, had affected districts 1, 2, and 3 (the accident occurred in district 2) earlier on June 19 and 20, 1998. During the course of the night and morning hours, thunderstorms developed rapidly and moved across parts of the turnpike. Torrential downpours and cloud-to-ground lightning were associated with these storms. The storms had produced local flooding and wind gusts of up to 40 mph.

[2] A full-service plaza (FSP) was about 13 miles away at MP 172.3.

[3] According to Greyhound policy, a driver is not supposed to pass a Greyhound bus that is pulled over without lights without checking to see whether the driver of the parked bus needs assistance.

Events Preceding the Accident

Table 1 reflects pertinent events leading up to the accident. The table was compiled using information from hotel registries, the driver's logbook entries, the accident bus' voice response unit (VRU),[4] and its engine's electronic control module (ECM).[5]

According to Greyhound officials, the busdriver's wife and grandchild boarded the bus in Philadelphia to ride with him on the his last trip before retirement. The Safety Board interviewed two other Greyhound drivers who had spoken to the accident driver at his next stop in Harrisburg. One of the interviewed drivers said that the accident driver appeared to be content with retiring, seemed normal, and did not seem tired or anything out of the ordinary.

An off-duty Pennsylvania State Police (PSP) trooper in a private vehicle reported that a few minutes before the accident on June 20, 1998, he was en route to Pittsburgh on the turnpike near the Tuscarora Tunnel. He recalled that when he entered the tunnel (MP 187.03) he noticed a Greyhound bus ahead of him in the right lane and that he was a short distance behind the bus when it exited the tunnel (MP 186.04). The State trooper stated that when both vehicles were about 500 to 1,000 feet beyond the tunnel, he started to pass the bus and saw it drift to the right, across the edge line, about half the width of the bus. He observed the bus correct back into the right lane and then drift left toward the center line. He said that when he was even with the driver's side window, he looked at the driver and saw a white male. The State trooper stated that the bus was traveling between 60 and 65 mph at that time. He said that he did not observe anything else unusual and continued on to Pittsburgh.

Emergency Response

The initial 911 cellular call from the occupant of a truck at the scene to the Hustontown (Fulton County) fire and rescue "dispatch"[6] was received about 4:11 a.m. by an emergency medical technician (EMT) at a local ambulance service.[7] According to the EMT, he obtained all the pertinent information from the 911 caller in about 3 minutes. He immediately contacted the turnpike dispatch center in Highspire, Pennsylvania,[8] which then dispatched emergency medical services, fire companies, and the PSP at 4:16 a.m.

---

[4] A computerized communication system used by Greyhound and its drivers. (See Greyhound Oversight section in this report for more information.)

[5] A semiconductor unit for controlling ignition timing and other parameters in an engine management system. (See Engine Electronic Control Module section for more information.)

[6] Fulton County does not have a 24-hour 911 emergency dispatch communications center; therefore, 911 calls for Fulton County fire and rescue assistance are transferred to a local number (used as the "emergency number" for the county). Calls to this local number are simultaneously channeled to four different locations: the Hustontown Volunteer Fire Department, a local ambulance service (which is where the EMT received the initial call), a local garage, and the Fulton County Medical Center.

[7] Approximate time based on receiver's attempt to recall time he looked at his watch.

[8] The standard procedure when an accident occurs on the turnpike.

Table 1. Events preceding the accident.

Shift Number	Date	Location	Events Preceding the Accident	Source	Comments
	June 16	Pittsburgh	Checked into hotel 2 45 p m	Hotel registry	
Day 1 of 4 day shift	June 17		Checked out of hotel 1 07 a m	Hotel registry	
			On duty not driving* 1 00 a m to 2 00 a m	Busdriver log	
			On duty driving** 2 00 a m to 6 00 a m	Busdriver log	
		Harrisburg	On duty not driving 6 00 a m to 6 30 a m	Busdriver log	
			On duty driving 6 30 a m to 8 30 a m	Busdriver log	
		Philadelphia	On duty not driving 8 30 a m to 9 30 a m	Busdriver log	
			On duty driving 9 30 a m to 12 00 p m	Busdriver log	
		New York City	On duty not driving 12 00 p m to 12 30 p m	Busdriver log	Driver logs indicated 8 5 hours driving 3 hours on duty not driving and 12 5 hours off duty
			Off duty*** 12 30 p m to 1 30 a m		
Day 2 of 4 day shift	June 18		On duty not driving 1 30 a m to 2 30 a m	Busdriver log	
			On duty driving 2 30 a m to 5 00 a m	Busdriver log	
		Philadelphia	On duty not driving 5 00 a m to 5 30 a m	Busdriver log	
			On duty driving 5 30 a m to 12 00 p m	Busdriver log	
		Pittsburgh	On duty not driving 12 00 p m to 12 30 p m	Busdriver log	Driver logs indicated 9 hours driving 1 5 hours on duty not driving and 11 5 hours off duty This is the last driver log entry found The driver made a VRU entry at 1 04 p m
			Checked into hotel 1 30 p m	Hotel registry	
Day 3 of 4 day shift			Checked out of hotel 10 05 p m	Hotel registry	
			Departed Pittsburgh 11 33 p m	VRU	The VRU was used to reconstruct events in the absence of driver logs but it could not be used to identify on and off duty times
	June 19	Philadelphia	Arrived Philadelphia 5 35 a m	VRU	
			Not driving 5 35 a m to 6 07 a m	VRU	
		New York City	Arrived New York City 8 56 a m	VRU	
			Checked into hotel 11 30 a m	Hotel registry	
Day 4 of 4 day shift			Checked out of hotel 8 30 p m	Hotel registry	
			Departed New York City 9 08 p m	VRU	
		Philadelphia	Arrived Philadelphia 11 58 p m	VRU	
			Not driving 11 58 p m to 12 35 a m	VRU	The ECM indicated that the bus was idling from 12 00 a m to 12 45 a m
	June 20	Harrisburg	Arrived Harrisburg 2 40 a m	VRU	The ECM indicated that the bus was driven from 12 45 a m to 2 30 a m
			Not driving 2 40 a m to 2 57 a m	VRU	The ECM indicated that the bus was idling from 2 30 a m to 3 00 a m
			Departed Harrisburg 2 57 a m	VRU	
		Burnt Cabins	Accident at 4 05 a m	VRU	The ECM indicated that the bus was driven from 3 00 a m to about 4 00 a m

* Title 49 *Code of Federal Regulations* (CFR) Part 395 2 defines on duty not driving as all time from beginning work or being in readiness for work and until being relieved from work or responsibilities

** Title 49 CFR Part 395 2 defines driving as all time spent at the driving controls of a commercial motor vehicle in operation

*** Title 49 CFR Part 395 8(h)(1) defines off duty as time not performing any work activity for the carrier or other compensated work

After notifying the turnpike dispatch center, he contacted the Hustontown Volunteer Fire Department and was informed that the accident had occurred in the Metal Township (Franklin County) Fire and Rescue Company call box area.[9] Metal Township is the closest fire and rescue facility to the accident site. (The Hustontown Fire Department then "stood down" as primary responding department.) The EMT next reached the Franklin County dispatch center and was instructed to dispatch the Hustontown Fire Department, which arrived first on scene at 4:22 a.m. The Metal Township firefighters arrived on scene shortly thereafter. The Metal Township fire chief, as the first senior ranking fire officer in the jurisdiction to arrive, assumed the role of incident commander (IC) for fire and rescue operations at the accident site. The first responding senior ranking PSP trooper was the IC for the turnpike and was responsible for the highway, highway safety, and accident investigation.

In addition to the above agencies, responders to the accident included Chambersburg Hospital (Franklin County) ambulances, the Cumberland Valley (Cumberland County) Hose Company, the Fannet-Metal Township (Franklin County) Fire Company, Huntingdon County, the Maryland State Police medivac helicopter, the Mercersburg (Fulton County) Fire Department, the Pleasant Hall (Fulton County) Fire Company, Waynesboro Hospital (Franklin County) advance life support ambulances, and the West End (Cumberland County) Fire and Rescue. (See figure 3 for the locations of emergency response departments.)

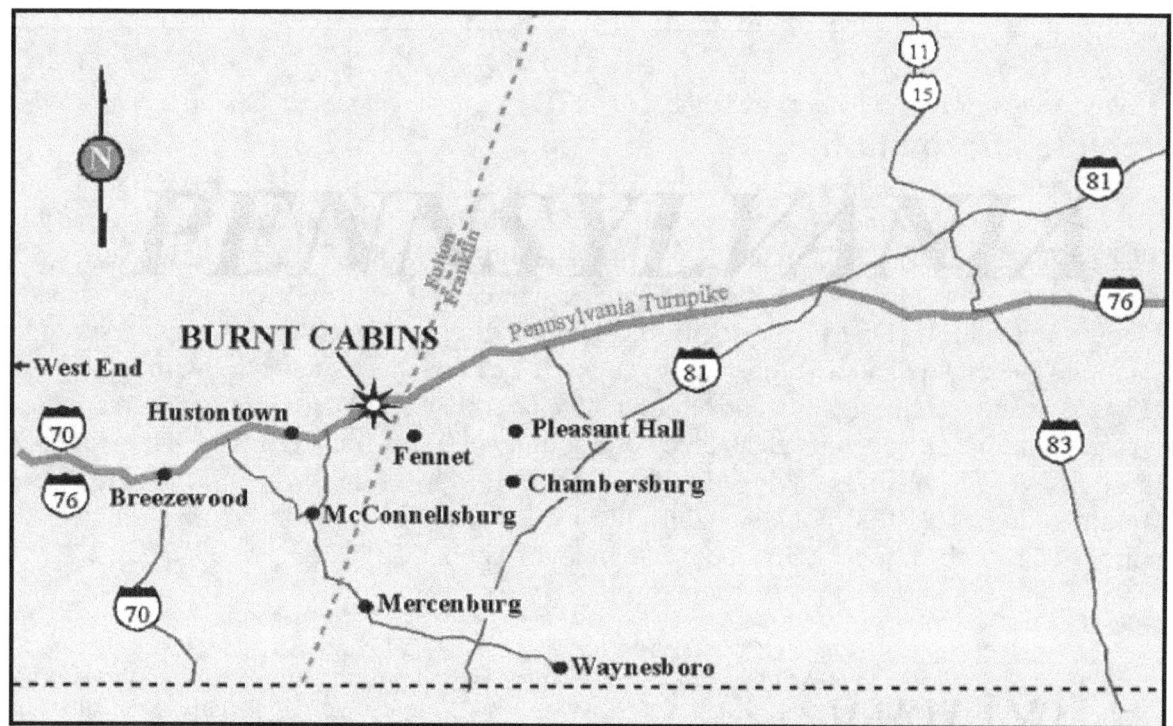

Figure 3. Locations of emergency response departments.

---

[9] A box card assignment set up exists for turnpike accidents. This assignment is a special area covered on the turnpike (Metal Township has the 2176 box) in which a prearranged number of units are to go to a specific accident.

Injuries

A total of 19 injured people were transported to three hospitals. One of the injured bus passengers expired upon arrival at the hospital. One bus passenger sustained serious injuries, including brain contusions; skull, pelvic, and torso fractures; and multiple lacerations; 15 bus passengers received minor injuries involving multiple contusions, lacerations, and abrasions. The two occupants of the TransAm truck sustained serious and minor injuries.

Table 2 is based on injury criteria[10] of the International Civil Aviation Organization, which the Safety Board uses in accident reports for all transportation modes. (See appendix C for an injury table based on the Abbreviated Injury Scale of the Association for the Advancement of Automotive Medicine.)

Table 2. Injuries.

Injuries	Drivers	Bus Passengers	Truck Occupants	Total
Fatal	1	6	0	7
Serious	0	1	1	2
Minor	0	15	1	16
None	0	0	1	1
Total	1	22	3	26

Vehicle Information

Motor Coach Industries Corporation of Pembina, North Dakota, manufactured the 47-passenger coach in September 1997. It was equipped with a Detroit Diesel Series 50, 8.5 liter, electronically controlled diesel engine, which was outfitted with a Detroit Diesel Electronic Controls (DDEC) model III ECM, which limited the maximum engine speed to 70 mph. The engine had a Jacobs engine brake.[11] The coach was outfitted with an Allison B500, 6-speed, electronically controlled, double overdrive, automatic transmission, which was programmed through its electronic control unit (ECU) to limit gear usage to gears one through five. The bus was equipped with a Rockwell/Meritor dual wheel drive axle (gross weight rating of 22,000 pounds) with an air spring design suspension that utilized air springs, shock absorbers, radius rods, and an antisway bar.

---

[10] Title 49 *Code of Federal Regulations* (CFR) 830.2 defines *fatal injury* as "Any injury which results in death within 30 days of the accident." It defines *serious injury* as an injury that "(1) Requires hospitalization for more than 48 hours, commencing within 7 days from the date the injury was received; (2) results in a fracture of any bone (except simple fractures of fingers, toes, or nose); (3) causes severe hemorrhages, nerve, or tendon damage; (4) involves any internal organ; or (5) involves second or third degree burns, or any burn affecting more than 5 percent of the body surface."

[11] A vehicle retarder system that modifies the engine valve timing to enable the engine to provide compression braking to augment the vehicle foundation brake system.

The coach was equipped with an S-cam air-actuated mechanical brake system. Greyhound maintenance records indicated that the brakes were last inspected on June 17, 1998. A visual inspection of the brake drums and system revealed no signs of cracking, contamination, defects, or deficiencies. Inspection brake applications were made using 95 pounds of air pressure per square inch supplied from an outside air source, and the brakes functioned as designed.

Engine Electronic Control Module

Safety Board investigators removed the ECM, and Detroit Diesel Corporation (Detroit Diesel) technicians extracted the data contained in the ECM. A printed "Engine Usage Profile" report of the data was provided to the Safety Board. The Detroit Diesel technicians enabled the optional "data pages" recording capability of the ECM, which had not previously been activated. According to Detroit Diesel, the data pages option on the DDEC III models, such as this one, requires a one-time activation fee; on the newer DDEC IV ECMs, this option is standard. In the inactive condition, the data pages information was still being captured but could be accessed only by the manufacturer.

At the time of the data extraction, the ECM's time clock was in error and read "10/22/85 14:08:10" when power to the ECM was disconnected. The date in the data file was adjusted to June 20, 1998, and the time was adjusted according to the point of power loss and approximate time of the accident. The information retrieved by Detroit Diesel from the equipment was used by the Safety Board to reconstruct the Greyhound driver's driving activity.

The information accessed from the ECM data pages indicated that, on the day of the accident, the coach was idling motionless from 12:00 to 12:45 a.m.[12] The bus was driven from 12:45 until 2:30 a.m. and idled motionless until about 3:00 a.m. It was driven again from 3:00 a.m. until the ECM stopped recording at approximately 4:00 a.m.

The ECM data also indicated that the bus had been operated at speeds as high as 76 mph on the day of the accident[13] and as high as 90 mph during the previous 90 days. Safety Board investigators were unable to determine the exact dates and operators of the occurrences due to the characteristics of the data pages printout. Fifteen instances were recorded in which the coach's speed ranged between 80 and 90 mph, and 34 instances were recorded in which the coach's speed ranged between 71 and 80 mph.[14] Hard brake[15] data for the day of the accident indicated that between 12:00 p.m. on June 19 and about

---

[12] All times are approximations based on the ECM *Engine Usage Profile Report*.

[13] The speed limit for the turnpike is 65 mph.

[14] The DDEC III ECM sampling rate of 10 times per second and resolution of ± 0.5 mph are dictated by the Society of Automotive Engineers J1587 standards. The speed given by the ECM can be higher than actual values due to tread wear. The accident coach had relatively new tires on the drive axle (approximately 0.1875-inch reduction in tire radius). As a result, actual speeds would be approximately 0.6 mph and 0.8 mph higher than the corresponding ECM speeds of 76 mph and 89.7 mph. A study of a DDEC III ECM on a similarly equipped bus was performed by Safety Board staff to evaluate its accuracy. Both speed and hard braking were found to be recorded within the accuracy expected.

[15] Defined by Detroit Diesel as a deceleration greater than 7 mph per second.

4:00 a.m. on June 20, the coach experienced two hard brake applications. The coach was driven on 13 of the 15 days immediately before the accident. The average high speed recorded for the 13 days was 78 mph, with a total of 14 hard brake applications.

According to Greyhound's senior vice president of operations, in June 1998, Greyhound was operating about 2,000 coaches, of which approximately 370 were equipped with either a DDEC III or IV ECM unit. ECM information was extracted during routine preventative maintenance strictly to ensure that the governed speed of the buses had not been tampered with and to monitor fuel consumption. He stated that, other than this use, Greyhound did not recognize a need for using the data pages recording options that were available because as of January 1998, Greyhound was operating only about 300 coaches with DDEC units. In August 1999, Greyhound was operating about 2,200 coaches of which approximately 900 were equipped with the units. Greyhound projects that around April 2000, the company may be operating about 1,300 coaches with DDEC III and IV ECM units. Greyhound has tentative plans to have older engines remanufactured by Detroit Diesel and equipped with DDEC III ECM units.

As of November 1999, Greyhound had not instituted a program to use the available ECM information in the oversight of driver operating habits.

Transmission Electronic Control Unit

The ECU was removed from the bus, and the Allison Transmission Corporation assisted the Board in its analysis. The ECU was not equipped to save vehicle speed, engine or transmission revolutions per minute, gear position, or torque or load percentages; therefore, these data could not be obtained.

Damage

The coach sustained substantial front-end damage and intrusion. (See figure 4.) Maximum right frontal intrusion was measured about 8 1/3 feet in the area of the floor line. The right front wheel assembly had been displaced rearward approximately 1 1/2 feet. The front bumper had been separated from the vehicle. The lower right front of the vehicle was displaced rearward about 1 3/4 feet and skewed upward approximately 1 foot. The roof along the right side had been displaced rearward 2 3/4 feet and was skewed downward. Maximum left frontal intrusion had occurred in the area of the windows; rearward displacement was about 9 feet. The left front leading edge of the roof was displaced rearward 2 feet and was skewed down and inward. The area of the front bumper mounts was displaced rearward 2 feet. Cutting tool-type damage was observed on the left side near the third and fourth windows with the cut section of the body panel pulled downward. The left front wheel assembly had been displaced rearward approximately 1 inch.

The coach's windshield was destroyed. The wiper arms were in the off position, as were the left and right windshield wiper control knobs. The steering wheel had been displaced rearward approximately 5.75 feet. The driver seat was not in place due to crush deformation rearward to the second row of passenger seats. (See figure 5.)

Figure 4. Exterior of damaged accident bus.

Figure 5. Interior left-side (driver) crush damage.

The coach was equipped with seven top-hinged emergency exit side windows on each side, excluding the driver's side windows. The passenger windows were 54 inches wide by 30 inches high. At the time of inspection, the first through third windows (front to rear) on the left side were missing; the fourth through seventh windows were intact and operational as emergency exits. On the right side, the first window was missing, the second was shattered, and the remaining windows were intact. The third window did not operate as an exit due to damage; the fourth window sustained structural damage and did not close, and its exit handle was blocked by a seat back. The remaining windows were operational as exits.

The coach had 11 rows of passenger seats, including the three-seat bench in the rear, which was intact. On the left side of the bus, the row-two seats were severely deformed, and the seats from rows three through five were found in the luggage compartment under the bus body. The row-six aisle seatback sustained inward deformation, while the row-seven aisle seat was rotated clockwise 10 degrees. The row-eight seatback cushions showed no evidence of impact marks, and the row-nine window seatback cushion was broken. At row 10, impact marks were on the aisle seatback cushions. On the right side of the bus, the passenger loading door was missing due to crush damage, which extended rearward to row two (see figure 6), and was found in the lower luggage compartment. Row three was crushed rearward into row four. From row 4 rearward through row 11, the seat frames were intact with some deflection of the seatback cushions. The window seats in rows four through eight were pushed forward and outward, with deformation to the rear of the seat below the level of seatback. Rows 9 through 10 were found relatively intact, without rear seatback deformation.

Busdriver Information

The 61-year-old busdriver held a valid Class B Pennsylvania commercial drivers' license (CDL) with passenger endorsement. The license was renewed on October 16, 1996, and had an expiration date of December 31, 2000.

The busdriver had been employed by Trailways Incorporated (Trailways) from April 1973 to August 1987, at which time Trailways merged with Greyhound. He had reported 32 years of busdriver experience on his Greyhound employment application. The busdriver listed his assignments with Trailways as dispatcher, busdriver, maintenance supervisor, and terminal manager. No records were available from the busdriver's employment with Trailways. Since the merger, the busdriver had been employed as a full-time driver with Greyhound. Before his current assignment to the Pittsburgh terminal, he had been assigned to the Philadelphia terminal from September 1996 to April 1997 and to the Pittsburgh terminal from June to September 1996. Other Greyhound duty stations listed were Camden, New Jersey; New York City; and Washington, D.C.

The busdriver had been assigned to the Pittsburgh Greyhound terminal since April 1997. He had bid and been selected in February 1998 for his present scheduled route, which he had driven weekly up to the time of the accident. The busdriver worked a 4-days-on

Figure 6. Interior right-side loading door and seat damage.

with 2-days-off cycle. His roundtrip schedule included driving from the Pittsburgh terminal to the New York City Port Authority (trip no. 1350) and from New York City to Pittsburgh (trip no. 1369). The busdriver was in the 4th day of the cycle and on trip no. 1369 when the accident occurred.

The busdriver's routine was to drive about 300 miles to Pittsburgh from Boothwyn, Pennsylvania, just south of Philadelphia. Greyhound files had the driver's recorded home address as Boothwyn. He usually checked into a hotel in Pittsburgh in the afternoon and checked out about 10 hours later. He then reported to the terminal, from which he departed on his scheduled trip.

Medical

Greyhound records revealed that during a March 1993 physical examination, the busdriver was diagnosed with hypertension and prescribed medication to control it. Records from his most recent physical examination, conducted on October 10, 1996, indicated that his blood pressure was normal. (No evidence was found to indicate that he was taking medication for hypertension at the time of the accident.) The busdriver's current medical examiner's certificate was also issued on October 10, 1996, and would have expired on October 9, 1998.

The busdriver received his last eye examination on November 1, 1996; at that time, his optometrist reported that his corrected vision was 20/25 in both eyes. The busdriver's medical certificate required him to wear corrective lenses while operating a vehicle. However, the busdriver had a valid Pennsylvania driver's license that permitted him to operate vehicles without corrective lenses. The State requires an eye examination only at the time the license is issued. Safety Board investigators were unable to determine whether the busdriver was wearing corrective lenses when the accident occurred.

On November 10, 1997, the busdriver visited his family physician complaining of nonradiating left-sided chest pain when at rest, short-term memory loss, and irritability. He also complained, as noted on the summary sheet from the visit, that he was limited to 10 hours driving per day but sometimes drove as much as 18 hours,[16] had trouble sleeping, and woke after only 3 to 4 hours of sleep. His physician ordered complete blood work, an electrocardiogram (EKG), and a Thallium stress test[17] for him. No abnormalities were found during the examination except for slightly elevated cholesterol levels.

According to the busdriver's sons, their father had a sinus condition for which he had surgery in the 1970s. They said that he took an over-the-counter decongestant medication daily.

Training

According to Greyhound, since 1992 all driver candidates have had to attend a 7-week structured initial training course, which includes classroom studies and behind-the-wheel instruction. Greyhound restructured its training program in response to Safety Board recommendations issued in 1992.[18] Because the accident driver began his employment with Greyhound before the implementation of this training requirement, he did not receive the training.

In addition, according to Greyhound, all drivers are required to attend an 8- to 10-hour in-service training program every 2 years. This program addresses several driving topics, including, but not limited to, fatigue, inclement driving conditions, and seasonal driving techniques. The driver refresher program has been in place since November 1997; according to the Greyhound director of training, as of November 1999, all drivers have received the driver refresher training. Greyhound stated that some type of refresher training has always been administered in the past, as well as an annual program about driving in inclement weather. The accident driver's personnel file did not contain any documentation of in-service training.

---

[16] Safety Board investigators were unable to verify whether he was referring to bus driving time only or was including driving his personal vehicle.

[17] A test performed, using a treadmill, to evaluate changes in EKG and blood distribution in the heart brought on by exercise.

[18] National Transportation Safety Board. 1992. *Greyhound Run-off-the-Road Accidents, Donegal, Pennsylvania, June 26, 1991, and Caroline, New York, August 3, 1991.* Highway Accident Report NTSB/HAR-92-01. Washington, DC.

Drivers returning to work after an extended leave of 30 days or more are required, according to Greyhound, to attend a 1-day driver refresher course, which may include a road test. The company stated that the purpose of the course is to reiterate safe driving techniques, driving skills, and Greyhound's service policies and to highlight the topics presented in the initial training course. Safety Board investigators did not discover, nor did Greyhound provide to investigators, any manual, course syllabus, or support documentation for refresher training.

In December 1992, after an absence of more than 30 days, the accident driver satisfactorily completed refresher training with a road test. The remarks section of the documentation noted that he "could use a refresher in about 3 to 6 months";[19] however, no documentation was found to indicate that such follow-up training was administered during that period. After returning to work from sick leave, the accident driver did again satisfactorily complete refresher training with a road test in January 1995. No documentation was located that described either the content or the duration of the training.

According to Greyhound, a driver refresher course may also be administered to drivers who have been involved in an accident or have received driving complaints. Although referred to as a refresher course, the curriculum and length differ from the above-described refresher course; the course is specifically designed to address the actions that caused the accident or the complaint. The accident driver's personnel file contained two forms for a "notice of personnel record entry" indicating his involvement in two preventable accidents[20] on November 19, 1995, and December 26, 1996. The 1995 accident involved another vehicle. The 1996 accident involved a "fixed object where he struck a parked car," and the personnel entry form stated that "due to the seriousness of the above accident, you are hereby required to take a 2-day refresher course." No other documents were found in the file indicating whether the accident driver had attended or successfully completed any refresher courses for these occurrences.

All training that each employee receives, according to Greyhound policy,[21] is documented in the individual driver's personnel file. A random review of 40 personnel and driver qualification files by Safety Board investigators revealed that 13 files did not contain the company-required documentation, that one driver with 20 years of service had only one entry for manual transmission training, and that another driver with 18 years of service had no training entries.

Driving Record

A review of the busdriver's personnel record revealed three speeding violations, one each in November 1989, February 1992, and August 1994. Records indicate that the

---

[19] Safety Board investigators and Greyhound officials were unable to determine the source of this comment.

[20] Defined by the Federal Highway Administration as an accident that (1) involves a commercial motor vehicle; (2) includes a fatality, injury, or damage requiring a vehicle be towed; and (3) could have been averted but for an act, or failure to act, by the motor carrier or driver.

[21] Policy 68: "It is the policy of this company to document all formal training attended by or provided to employees, contractors, and others."

1992 and 1994 speeding violations occurred while he was operating a bus. The 1992 ticket was issued for traveling 77 mph in a 55-mph zone, for which Greyhound suspended him for 5 days. The busdriver received a written warning from Greyhound for the 1989 speeding violation.

The busdriver's personnel records also revealed that including the two accidents mentioned above, he was involved in two accidents in 1990; one in 1991; one in 1993; three in 1995, one of which resulted in an unsafe-lane-change violation; and two in 1996. All of these accidents occurred while he was operating a bus. Although present in the driver's personnel files, these accidents do not appear in the Pennsylvania motor vehicle records for the driver.

Additionally, the busdriver's personnel records disclosed that he had received 5-day suspensions in 1989 and 1990 for "refusing an assignment" and for "operating a bus without authorization," respectively. Two warnings were noted in the record for "failing to show up for work" on July 23, 1990, and December 24, 1993. He also received a 2-day suspension for "failing to fill out a passenger list after an accident" and a 1-day suspension for "log violations" in 1995.

Greyhound has a safe driver award recognition program; the awards are presented annually. To qualify for a safety award, a driver must complete 6 consecutive months of driving without a preventable accident. A driver may obtain subsequent safety awards by completing 12 consecutive months of driving without a preventable accident. Traffic violations do not preclude awards. According to Greyhound, the accident busdriver had received a 6-month safe driving award in 1988 and 1-year awards in 1990 through 1993.[22]

Complaints About the Driver

A passenger who said she frequently traveled on Greyhound between Philadelphia and Pittsburgh contacted Safety Board investigators after the accident. She reported that, in December 1997 and January 1998, she rode a Greyhound bus that was driven by the accident driver. She said that, during these trips, she saw the busdriver "nod off" as he drove the bus. During the December trip, she then observed the bus drift to the right onto the grooved pavement of the right shoulder. She said that the sound of the tires on the grooves awakened the driver and that he steered to the left back onto the roadway. The passenger reported that the busdriver repeated the same behavior several more times during the trip. She believed that he must have fallen asleep at least once every hour.

The passenger reported that, on one occasion, she informed two Greyhound supervisors at the Pittsburgh terminal of her observations. The passenger said that the supervisors displayed an "unconcerned attitude" and that one supervisor said of the driver falling asleep, "don't they all."

---

[22] The records of other interstate carriers' busdrivers are not stored in a central repository. Individual companies retain their drivers' records, making it difficult to obtain information to compare the accident driver's record with other interstate carrier busdrivers. However, according to the Greyhound safety director, the accident busdriver's record was a little below average when compared with the other Greyhound busdrivers' records.

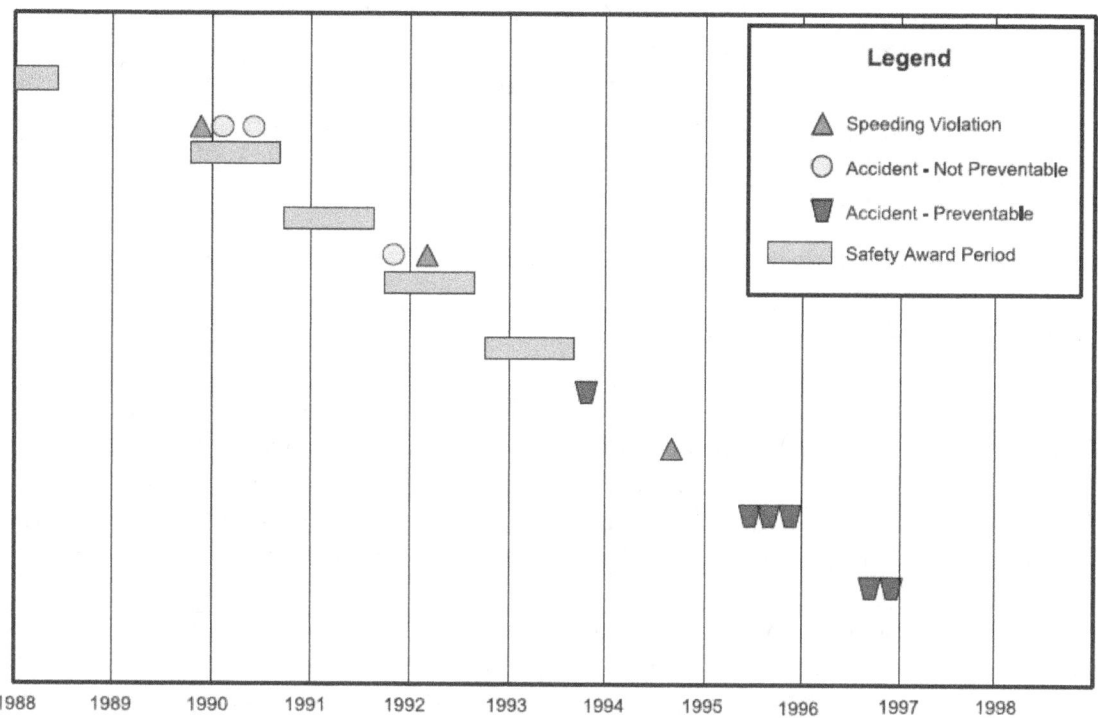

Figure 7. Chart of busdriver's driving record.

On a third occasion in January 1998, this passenger again boarded a bus with the accident driver. She said that she asked him whether he was going to fall asleep during the trip and that he became angry, ejected her from the bus, and escorted her to a supervisor. The passenger reported that the busdriver told the supervisor that she had a "smart mouth" and that he would not permit her to ride on his bus. She noted that another passenger left the bus at the same time. After she filed a written report with the supervisor about her observations on the other trips, the supervisor placed her and the other passenger on another bus.

After the Burnt Cabins accident, the passenger recognized the busdriver from a photograph on a news report. She stated that she then attempted to notify Greyhound but was disconnected. She said that on a second attempt, she talked to a reservationist with Greyhound who referred her to another number, which she did not call.

According to Greyhound's vice president of driver operations, when a complaint about a driver is received, whether oral or written, it is forwarded to the driver's immediate supervisor for a follow-up investigation. In the case of an oral complaint, the supervisor will request that it be provided in writing. The supervisor will investigate and document in the driver's personnel file whether the complaint is founded or unfounded. The supervisor may discuss the findings of the investigation with the driver or take other action, following the guidelines of progressive discipline, which can range from an oral warning to suspension without pay or termination.

Although the vice president of driver operations advised the Safety Board about the above procedures, Greyhound has no written policy for documenting and processing driver complaints. Greyhound had no record of the complaints about the accident busdriver, nor did the employees involved in the situation recall the incidents. Greyhound's 1-800-SAFEBUS program[23] does include a written policy for processing complaints against drivers.

Motor Carrier Information

Greyhound operates 24 hours a day, 7 days a week, as an interstate carrier of passengers providing scheduled bus service within the continental United States, and it has limited operations in Canada and Mexico. Greyhound conducts special destination,[24] charter, and package services throughout its scheduled areas. Greyhound is registered with the Federal Highway Administration (FHWA) as an interstate carrier.

All scheduled Greyhound operations are monitored from a central location in Dallas, Texas. Greyhound has 11 driver operation and customer service districts that encompass 88 terminals to which drivers are assigned and report for work; driver supervisors are assigned to 61 of these terminals. In addition, passengers can be picked up or discharged at 1,530 bus stop locations. Greyhound travels approximately 254.6 million miles annually in scheduled passenger service.

At the time of the accident, Greyhound had a fleet of 2,155 motorcoaches; it owned 873 and leased 1,282 buses. The average age of the fleet was 6.11 years. Greyhound employed 4,121 drivers (4,013 full time and 108 part time). The average driver age and experience were 47 and 11 years, respectively.

Motor Carrier Oversight

To reduce accidents and ensure compliance with Federal regulations, according to Greyhound, it has in place a multifaceted oversight program that includes driver training, driver refresher training (every 2 years), a safety manual, driver supervision by field safety managers, safety managers riding with drivers, customer service feedback from passengers, and safety bulletins (at least one per month).

Greyhound policy 37 states, "The company is committed to the safety of its passengers and employees." A full-time safety director reports directly to the chief operating officer. A staff of 18 employees under the safety director is responsible for overseeing the drivers' 24-hour period of records of duty status (logs) and qualification

---

[23] See 1-800-SAFEBUS program section in this report for more details.

[24] Casinos, shows, and special events.

files and the alcohol and drug testing program and for preparing safety bulletins and coordinating safety meetings.

Greyhound reported that it generates an average of 4,200 driver logs per day. The log books are submitted monthly to an outside vendor, CommData, in Carrolton, Texas, for review, computer analysis for hours-of-service, and storage. The vendor provides Greyhound with log book hours-of-service discrepancies it discovers. Any hours-of-service discrepancies found by the vendor are forwarded to the safety director, who notifies the driver's supervisor for appropriate action.

In November 1998, the vendor notified Greyhound that of the 106,679 logs reviewed, 152 logs were found to have exceeded the 10-hour rule, 76 logs exceeded the 15-hour rule, and 115 logs exceeded the 70-hour rule.[25]

According to Greyhound, its drivers routinely have daily contact with company safety supervisors at the terminals and receive a monthly newsletter, which covers various safety topics. According to Greyhound and the drivers, management, drivers, and operational personnel participate in quarterly safety meetings. Each terminal has a bulletin board on which safety memos and posters provided by the safety department are to be displayed. Safety Board investigators examined posters and safety messages that, according to Greyhound, were previously displayed in terminals and are now retained in the safety department files.

Schedules

Greyhound reported that its schedules comply with Federal regulations and take into account such factors as the number of drivers located in specific cities, the location of maintenance facilities, the seniority of drivers, and the availability of dormitories or hotels when overnight stays are built into the runs. Greyhound and union representatives review the schedules or runs at least four times a year to ensure that they meet Federal and company standards.

A regular driver, also known as a scheduled run driver, is one who drives a scheduled run (tour) with specified stops. The schedules specify a departure and an arrival time at each terminal. The drivers are required to sign in (on-duty-not-driving), usually 30 minutes before their first departure time and to sign off (off-duty), usually 30 minutes after their last arrival time. Some schedules require a driver to pick up or drop off a bus at a garage away from the terminal, requiring an additional 15 to 30 minutes of on-duty time.

A contractual agreement between Greyhound and the Amalgamated Transit Union establishes the Greyhound drivers' compensation rate. Greyhound predetermines the compensation rate for each tour based on the tour scheduled driving time. Drivers are contractually obligated, without further compensation, to perform pre- and posttrip bus

---

[25] Title 49 CFR Part 395.3 prohibits motor carriers who operate 7 days a week from permitting or requiring any driver to drive more than 10 hours following 8 consecutive hours off-duty, or for any period after having been on-duty 15 hours following 8 consecutive hours off-duty, or for any period after accumulating 70 hours on-duty in any period of 8 consecutive days.

inspections, load baggage, fuel buses, and take tickets; for scheduled rest stops of 30 minutes or longer; and for delays of up to 45 minutes upon completion of the trip. Drivers receive additional compensation if the schedule requires them to transport the bus to a garage that is separate from the terminal and if they are more than 45 minutes late (compensation begins after the first 45 minutes).[26]

Policy 37 in the Greyhound safety manual states, "A regular driver's commute time plus the on-duty not driving/driving time of the run must be 15 hours or less. If a regular driver's commute time plus the on-duty not driving/driving time is greater than 15 hours he will not be permitted to bid the run." The commute time, according to the Greyhound safety director, is considered only when the driver is reporting to drive the run and not when the driver is returning home after driving the run.

The accident driver's tour required him to sign on-duty 30 minutes before the scheduled departure time and sign off-duty 35 minutes after arrival time. The scheduled time for the tour was 11 hours 30 minutes. Safety Board investigators drove at the posted speed limits from Boothwyn (the accident driver's address) to Pittsburgh (the driver's home terminal), and the trip took 5 hours 30 minutes.

According to the vice president of driver operations, Greyhound permits drivers to bid on runs by seniority and has no limit on the commute distance that scheduled run drivers can live from the terminal when they bid on a run. However, scheduled run drivers have to have a local address near the terminal or board location within 2 weeks of bid acceptance and are permitted to use dormitory facilities at the terminal for up to 30 days until they find living quarters. Living arrangements can be either permanent or temporary. Extra board drivers[27] are required to reside within 2 hours travel time of the terminal to which they report.

Greyhound has no written policies for establishing and maintaining a domicile address and does not require that records of a driver's domicile address be maintained. The accident driver's personnel and driver qualification file listed a Boothwyn address; no documents were found that listed his domicile address in the Pittsburgh area. Safety Board investigators found that, like the accident driver, other drivers in the Greyhound system are assigned to a terminal and use other facilities, such as hotels, that are away from their permanent residence.

Speeding

According to Greyhound, each bus in its fleet is equipped with an ECM that governs or restricts the bus operation to a maximum speed of between 68 and 70 mph. However, the ECM data downloaded from the accident bus indicated that the bus had

---

[26] In December 1998, a Safety Board investigator questioned the president of the Amalgamated Transit Union about scheduling and compensation for required safety inspections. According to the investigator, the union president responded that he did not know anything about this and terminated the telephone call by hanging up.

[27] Extra board drivers are drivers who are not assigned a regular scheduled trip but are available on-call, as needed for extra runs, charters, or in the absence of a regular driver.

traveled at speeds as high as 76 mph on the day of the accident and as high as 90 mph during the 90 days preceding the accident. Safety Board investigators, while driving the accident driver's route between New York City and Pittsburgh, observed Greyhound buses speeding as high as 86 mph and on occasion following other vehicles closely. They found that the buses did not travel faster than the governed speed on an upgrade or level road surface but did exceed the governed speed on a downgrade.

As a result of their observations, Safety Board investigators monitored Greyhound buses with radar, pacing them with a global positioning system mapping computer program. The monitoring was conducted throughout the United States from the terminals in Harrisburg; Pittsburgh; Denver, Colorado; Cincinnati, Ohio; Atlanta, Georgia; Nashville and Chattanooga, Tennessee; Seattle, Washington; Dallas; Milwaukee, Wisconsin; and Baltimore, Maryland. Safety Board investigators identified the number of each bus on 40 different trips and observed that all 40 drivers were speeding, 6 were following too closely, 5 made improper lane changes, and 10 disregarded red traffic signals. Five drivers exceeded 80 mph, one driver operated at 86 mph, and another driver traveled at 73 mph in a 40-mph construction zone. Greyhound was advised of the above findings and identified 35 of the 40 drivers.[28]

The Safety Board reviewed the logs of the 35 drivers and calculated average daily speeds from the log entries by dividing the miles driven by the duty hours driving. The findings varied and included three drivers who averaged 20 to 25 mph on a run, one driver who averaged 120 mph, and another driver who averaged 247 mph.

According to the Greyhound safety director, after the Safety Board observed the 40 buses speeding, Greyhound observed an additional 140 buses and found that 140 drivers exceeded the posted speed limit. The company, according to the Greyhound safety director, has begun a radar monitoring program of buses by safety managers. As of November 1999, Greyhound had five radar units and planned to acquire a sixth within another month.

Company policy, according to Greyhound, is, "if you are late, stay late," and its purpose is to reduce the drivers' need to speed. The drivers' performance evaluation does not address on-time arrival. Safety Board investigators interviewed 2 Greyhound drivers and received correspondence from 11 others on the issue of speeding. These drivers stated they often try to make up for lost time by speeding. The drivers indicated that ensuring passengers made connections with other buses was a reason for speeding. They said that the driver is normally the one who hears complaints about missed connections from passengers. The drivers also stated that when they depart late, they report that they arrive late, even if they arrive on time. They believe that if they are able to drive the trip in a shorter time, Greyhound will reduce the schedule time, thus reduce their pay. Safety Board investigators reviewed several Greyhound trip schedules and found that they could be met without exceeding the speed limit.

---

[28] Five drivers were not identified because of discrepancies in schedules and bus numbers.

Pre- and Posttrip Inspections

The *Federal Motor Carrier Safety Regulations* (FMCSR) list the vehicle parts that must be inspected by a driver before operating a bus. The driver of a commercial motor vehicle is to "be satisfied that the motor vehicle is in safe operating condition" and is prohibited from operating the vehicle if found in unsafe condition. The driver is also required to conduct a posttrip inspection of the vehicle daily and is directed to make a written report of the inspection and submit it to the carrier. Any defects found "that would likely affect the safety operation of the vehicle" must be corrected before the vehicle can be driven on a public roadway.

The accident bus was operated on two runs on June 19, one of which included the accident trip. The accident driver completed the Greyhound pre- and posttrip inspection reports for the accident bus for June 19, even though the accident occurred before the run was completed.

Accident Register

Title 49 *Code of Federal Regulations* (CFR) 390.15(b) requires that all carriers maintain an accident register for 1 year that records all reportable accidents involving the carriers' vehicles. A reportable accident is defined as one that involves (1) a fatality, (2) bodily injury requiring immediate medical treatment, or (3) one or more vehicles damaged to such an extent that towing is required. The accident register must contain the accident date, location, driver name, injuries, and fatalities and state whether hazardous materials, other than vehicle fuel, were involved and released.

A review of its accident register for January 1998 through October 1998 revealed that Greyhound had recorded 150 reportable accidents, which involved a total of 4 fatalities, 57 injuries, and 89 towed vehicles. Two errors were noted on the accident register. A traffic collision near Flagstaff, Arizona, on July 13, 1998, resulted in a fatality; the register recorded it as an injury accident. Then, a traffic accident at Mount Pocono, Pennsylvania, resulted in 10 injuries; the register listed it as a noninjury accident.[29] Safety Board investigators reported these errors to the Greyhound director of safety, who has informed the Safety Board that the accident register has been corrected.

Voice Response Unit

Since 1992, Greyhound has utilized the VRU, a computerized communication system, for busdrivers to transmit information to Greyhound management. The system employs between 100 and 120 lines to accommodate calls. According to Greyhound, 75 percent of the calls to the dispatch center are through the VRU system.

Greyhound operation requires drivers to enter their current terminal location through the VRU telephone keypad. Greyhound officials stated that as much as a 15-minute delay can occur from the time a driver arrives at a terminal and the time he

---

[29] Safety Board investigators determined the errors after reviewing the State police reports for the two accidents.

actually enters information into the VRU system. They said that the drivers' duties vary from terminal to terminal, which could delay the VRU transmission. Greyhound officials also reported that a through driver (one who is continuing his trip to another terminal to load or unload passengers) can do both the inbound and outbound call at the same time.

In addition, management uses the VRU system to call drivers to work, to notify drivers of run bid changes, to gather passenger counts for planning purposes, and to broadcast safety messages. The drivers can also use it to monitor the assignment board and to receive personal mailbox messages.

Mystery Rider Program

Under Greyhound's Mystery Rider Program, a compensated volunteer, usually a former Greyhound manager, randomly observes the company facilities, equipment, service, and schedule times and the driver skills and practices. On-board mystery riders[30] monitor busdrivers who have complaints lodged against them concerning their driving habits or customer service skills. Information obtained by a mystery rider is filed with management and placed in a driver's personnel file.

1-800-SAFEBUS

The 1-800-SAFEBUS program is described in the Greyhound safety manual as one of its driver safety check programs. The purpose of the program is to allow the public to report to the company, using a toll free telephone number, on driver performance, service, and driving behavior. According to Greyhound, a 1-800-SAFEBUS decal is displayed on the rear exterior of most Greyhound buses in the upper left-hand corner.

Greyhound currently contracts with an outside vendor, Fleetsafe, in Atlanta to service the program. At the time of the accident, the vendor was Safetynet, which was purchased by Fleetsafe in November 1998. The contract costs are based on the number of vehicles in the fleet so, according to Greyhound, it is important that each bus be identified with a 1-800-SAFEBUS decal.

When Fleetsafe receives a 1-800-SAFEBUS call, a telephone operator there has a script displayed on a computer screen to ensure that the proper information is obtained. According to Greyhound, when the vendor receives either a positive report or a complaint from an identified caller leaving a telephone number, it notifies the Greyhound safety department. If a complaint is received from an anonymous caller, the vendor will neither process the complaint nor notify Greyhound, and no further action is taken. Greyhound specifies this procedure because of prank anonymous complaints received in the past. At the time of the accident, the 1-800-SAFEBUS program operated by Safetynet provided similar service.

---

[30] According to the Greyhound safety director, the company had 10 mystery riders in 1999. Greyhound has no set schedule for the use of mystery riders, and their use varies from year to year. The director of safety was unable to determine how many times the mystery riders were used in 1999.

Greyhound policy requires its safety department to contact the caller and solicit further details. In the case of either a negative or positive report, a fax is forwarded to the driver's supervisor. All 1-800-SAFEBUS complaints are filed at the driver's home terminal and do not become part of the driver's personnel or qualification files. The supervisor may discuss the incident with the driver, institute a check ride with a supervisor or mystery rider, or do nothing. According to Greyhound, no discipline can directly result from a 1-800-SAFEBUS complaint; however, the complaint can lead to further Greyhound inquiry that may result in driver discipline. In addition, according to Greyhound, its safety department receives monthly 1-800-SAFEBUS reports containing the type and location of driver complaints. The safety department follows up with supervisors concerning disciplinary action to be taken for drivers who are repeatedly listed on the monthly reports.

Through the 1-800-SAFEBUS program, Fleetsafe also provides an emergency notification service to Greyhound. If a 1-800-SAFEBUS call is received indicating that a Greyhound bus is involved in an accident or needs assistance, the operators at Fleetsafe contact emergency services in that area and notify essential Greyhound management and safety personnel.

On July 15, 1998, a Safety Board investigator called 1-800-SAFEBUS and identified a bus traveling from Harrisburg that was speeding and following too closely and had disregarded a red light. The operator stated that it was unnecessary to provide a name or telephone number and that the information would be given to a Greyhound supervisor. Because of the operator's statement, the investigator did not leave a name or number. When Safety Board investigators conducted a review of company records in October 1998, no record of this call was found. According to Greyhound management, the operator should have solicited a name so that the call could have been processed further. Greyhound did advise the 1-800-SAFEBUS vendor, which was Safetynet at that time, of its phone operator's comments, but no additional information was obtained.

On August 6, 1998, a Safety Board investigator again called 1-800-SAFEBUS and identified a bus traveling from Cincinnati that was speeding, following too closely, and making sudden lane changes. The Safety Board investigator identified himself and provided his name and number to the operator. The 1-800-SAFEBUS incident report on file at Greyhound did not reflect the speeding complaint, no follow-up call was made to the Safety Board investigator, and no action was taken by Greyhound.

In October 1998, Safety Board investigators reviewed incidents reported to 1-800-SAFEBUS for April through September 1998. The term selected encompasses the time period before and after the accident. In April, May, June, July, August, and September, respectively, 2, 38, 343, 385, 354, and 213 incidents were reported. The low number of incidents reported in April, according to Greyhound, was the result of its own management and internal program changes.

During the investigation of this accident, Safety Board investigators and Greyhound managers randomly selected for review 3 of 1,186 driver incidents that had been reported to 1-800-SAFEBUS. The nature of the complaints and Greyhound's findings were:

1. rude and discourteous service. Call back made to complainant, and complaint referred to driver's supervisor. No further action indicated.

2. changing lanes and cutting off another motorist. Call back made to complainant, and incident report forwarded to driver's supervisor. Follow-up interview included explanation by driver and supervisor's comments to the driver. Documented with supervisor's recommendation for driver refresher if subsequent infractions occur. Form signed by supervisor, but not by driver.

3. unsafe lane change and improper passing. Call back made to complainant, and incident referred to supervisor. Follow-up included driver check ride, report of which indicated driver courteous and operating bus in safe manner. No further action taken.

Federal Motor Carrier Safety Ratings

Greyhound has been subject to several Office of Motor Carriers and Highway Safety (OMCHS) compliance reviews,[31] which have been conducted by the OMCHS or Texas. (See appendix D for information on Federal motor carrier ratings procedures.) The most recent review of Greyhound before this accident was done by the Texas Department of Public Safety (DPS) on July 16, 1997. The other safety compliance reviews were performed by the OMCHS in 1996, 1995, 1993 (twice), 1991, and 1989. All reviews resulted in satisfactory ratings. However, the FHWA made recommendations to Greyhound for improved safety in some of those reviews, as follows.

1997 Greyhound Compliance Review

After reviewing the data from the Texas DPS review (see table 3), the FHWA recommended to Greyhound that it conduct periodic internal reviews of its driver qualification files, hours-of-service controls, vehicle maintenance practices, accident analysis and reporting procedures, training, and other safety systems to ensure continued compliance with the FMCSRs.

---

[31] Title 49 CFR Part 385.3 defines "compliance review" as an on-site examination of motor carrier operations, such as drivers' hours of service, maintenance and inspection, driver qualification, CDL requirements, financial responsibility, accidents, hazardous materials, and other safety and transportation records, to determine whether a motor carrier meets the safety fitness standard.

Table 3. Greyhound 1997 compliance review.

Factors	Points	Violations
1 - General	0	None
2 - Driver	0	10 ---- section 382.413, failure to obtain drug/alcohol information from previous employer 02 ---- section 391.11(b)(8), no indication of road test 03 ---- section 391.23(a), no preemployment background check 01 ---- section 391.25, failure to review driver qualification file annually
A total of 156 driver records were checked. Because no violation was weighted as acute or critical, no points were assessed.		
3 - Operational	0	04 ---- section 395.3, hours-of-service
A total of 868 records were checked. This section is weighted as critical. A pattern of noncompliance equals 10 percent, or more, violations in records checked. Since the number of violations did not exceed 10 percent of the records checked, no points were assessed.		
4 - Vehicle	0	None
A total of 572 roadside vehicle inspections were reviewed. An out-of-service rate of 5.6 percent was determined. The 34-percent limit was not met; therefore, no points were assessed.		
5 - Hazardous Materials		Not Applicable
6 - Accidents	0	None
Greyhound recorded 61 reportable accidents in the 12 months before the review. (Greyhound vehicles, nationally, accumulated over 254.6 million miles in that time.) The accident rate was 0.24, which fell below the 0.3 criteria; therefore, no points were assessed.		

1996 Greyhound Compliance Review

In 1996 the OMCHS discovered 12 violations, 11 of which were logbook-related. It made the following recommendations:

1. Do not permit a person to drive after testing positive for controlled substances unless that person has been evaluated by a substance abuse professional.

2. Establish a system of control for driver hours-of-service to prevent hours-of-service violations and falsification of logbooks.

3. Do not dispatch drivers who do not have adequate hours-of-service available to complete the trip.

4. Verify hours-of-service records with supporting documents.

1995 Greyhound Compliance Review

In 1995, the safety compliance review identified 144 violations of the FMCSRs; 120 were drivers failing to forward logbook pages to the company within the required

13-day time limit, and 12 involved hours-of-service breaches. The FHWA made the following recommendations:

1. Ensure that all drivers are qualified and that complete driver employment files are maintained.

2. Ensure drivers receive a medical examination every 24 months.

3. Ensure that all drivers participate in preemployment, biennial, random, reasonable cause, and postaccident drug and alcohol screenings.

4. Maintain all required controlled substance testing records.

5. Do not permit employees who have tested positive for controlled substances to drive.

6. Require all drivers to prepare and submit accurate logbook entries within 13 days.

7. Implement a system of hours-of-service control and do not permit drivers to violate the 10-, 15-, and 70-hours-of-service rules.

8. Ensure that all vehicles are systematically repaired and maintained.

Highway Information

The multi-vehicle accident occurred in a marked emergency parking pull-off area adjacent to the straight and slightly uphill westbound lanes of the Pennsylvania Turnpike[32] at MP 184.9 in Huntingdon County, between the Fort Littleton interchange (13) at MP 179.5 and the Willow Hill interchange (14) at MP 188.6. This segment of the turnpike was constructed in 1940 and designated as Interstate 76 in 1956. (See figure 1.) The posted speed limit was 65 mph. According to turnpike traffic flow records, the average daily traffic between interchanges 13 and 14 was 19,033 vehicles (34 percent commercial) in 1997 and 20,278 vehicles (34 percent commercial) in 1998.

The turnpike consists of 506 miles of roadway, of which 360 miles are private, with 46 interchanges and 5 tunnels. The turnpike has 22 full-service plazas (FSPs).[33] The distance between these plazas is between 31 and 35 miles, depending on the direction of travel and the turnpike segment. Also, emergency call boxes line both sides of the turnpike at 1-mile intervals, providing motorists in need of assistance with an instant link to the turnpike's communications center in Highspire. A call box is located at MP 185.05 at the beginning of the emergency parking area.

---

[32] The Pennsylvania Turnpike Commission was created in May 1937 to construct, operate, and maintain a limited-access toll road.

[33] According to the Pennsylvania Turnpike Commission, Federal grants comprised 1.33 percent of its total revenues and receipts from June 1, 1998, through May 31, 1999. Federal funds are allocated to purchase equipment, such as variable message signs and other advanced electronic equipment, and are not used for highway construction or maintenance.

At the accident area, the roadway was straight with a 3-percent grade. The roadway had an asphaltic concrete surface with asphalt shoulders that were reportedly wet at the time the accident.[34] The cross section of the westbound roadway consisted of a 4.5-foot-wide left shoulder, two 12-foot-wide lanes with a 1.2-percent side slope, and an approximately 28-foot-wide right shoulder (emergency pull-off area) with a 4.2-percent side slope and a 45-degree embankment. The east and westbound traffic lanes were separated by 45-inch-high Jersey barriers. The lane markings were 15-foot-long painted white stripes at 25-foot intervals. The lane markings and the standard 4-inch solid yellow and white edge lines were all visible. At the accident site, the highway shoulder had rumble strips that were approximately 4 inches from the travel lane.

Tire marks, approximately 28 feet long, at the accident site had a departure angle from the roadway between 3 and 4 degrees. The tire marks started about 170 feet west of MP 185 (see figure 8). Approximately 39 feet of gouges and scrub marks were observed on the shoulder pavement, as well as an impact mark on the earthen embankment. In addition, 61-foot-long tire marks from the TransAm tractor-semitrailer's precollision parked position to its postcollision position were identified. The PSP surveyed the accident scene and the final rest positions of the accident vehicles.

Accident History at Site

Using Pennsylvania Turnpike Commission (Commission) accident reports, the Safety Board compiled a 5-year (January 1993 to December 1997) accident history of the area 1.5 miles in both directions from the accident site. During this period, 23 accidents occurred, of which 8 included injuries and 15 had property damage. No fatal accidents were reported.

Five of these accidents occurred at night; 18 occurred during daylight. One of the 18 daylight accidents occurred in the accident site emergency parking area. It involved a single vehicle and occurred during snowfall. Of the five night accidents, two involved more than one vehicle. One of these two involved a truck tractor that was rear-ended by a car in the roadway.

According to the Commission's records, the same 5-year period average fatal accident rate for the entire turnpike was 0.44 and the injury rate was 26.5 per 100-million vehicle miles. For the same period, the number of vehicles using the turnpike was approximately 118.97 million, and the miles driven were about 4.5 billion. Between 1993 and 1997, per 100-million vehicle miles, the fatal accident rate for the Nation's interstates and for rural interstates in Pennsylvania was 0.75 and 0.57, respectively.

---

[34] The off-duty State trooper who traveled through the scene moments before the accident and the investigating PSP reported no problems with visibility at the time of the accident. They said that, although it had been raining heavily earlier, the rain had stopped. Patches of damp areas remained on the roadway, but no standing water was present. All reported low-level fog, or what they interpreted as steam, rising about 2 or 3 feet from the road surface.

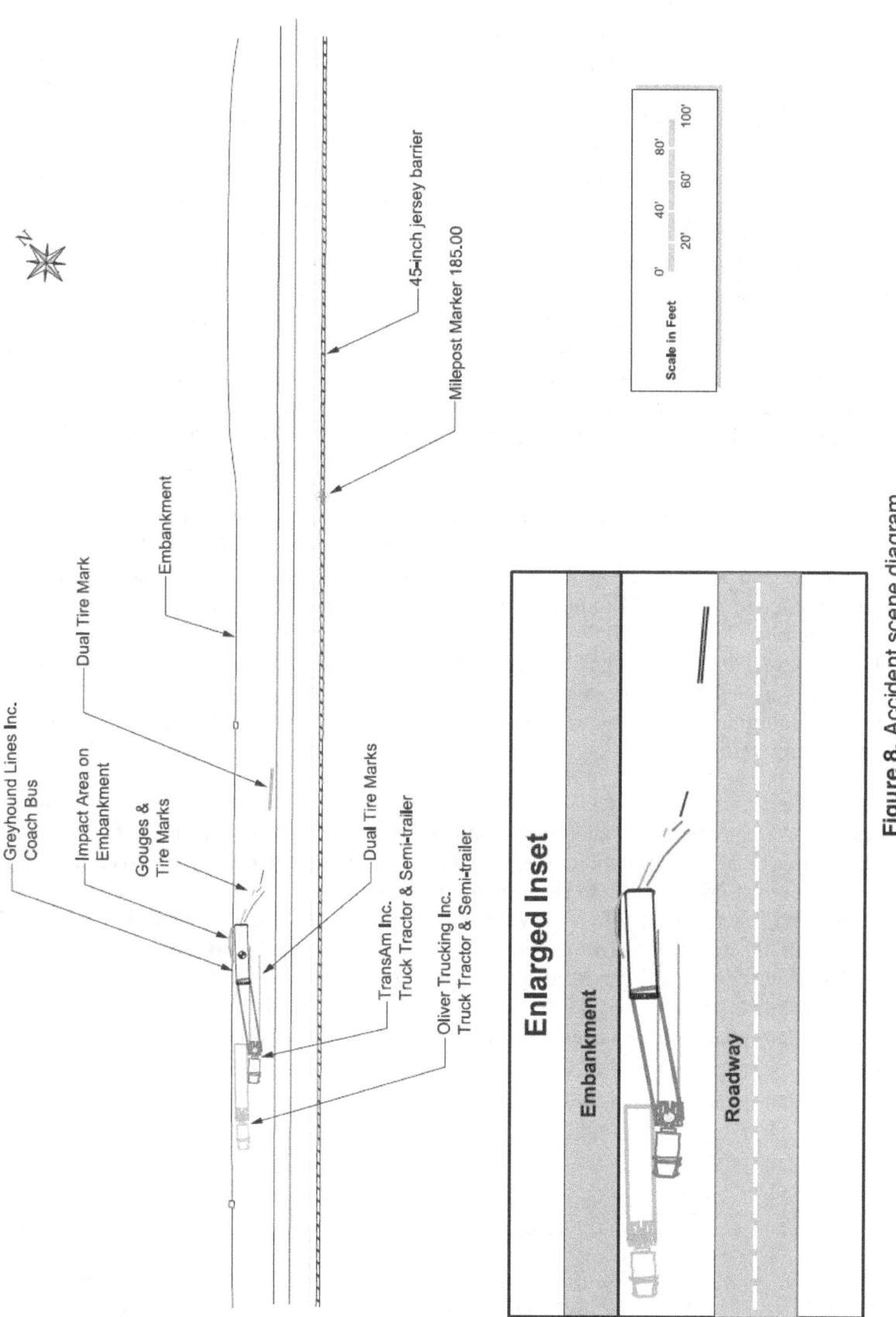

Figure 8. Accident scene diagram.

Pennsylvania Turnpike Pull-Off Areas

The turnpike has several different types and sizes of pull-off areas, both unmarked and marked emergency parking and picnic areas. The accident occurred at a marked emergency parking pull-off area about 13 miles from the next FSP (MP 172.3). The TransAm tractor semitrailer was parked 9 to 10 feet from the edge of the travel lane.

According to the Commission, the unmarked pull-off areas have evolved over time as a result of construction or maintenance equipment pulling off the travel lanes and shoulders onto these areas during roadway rehabilitation or snow removal procedures. The Commission advised that these areas were never intended to be used as emergency parking or picnic pull-off areas by the motoring public. The Commission has published guidelines[35] for the marked emergency parking and picnic areas that include having a minimum length of 200 and 300 feet, respectively; being on a level or downhill grade; and being on the inside of a horizontal curve with adequate sight distance. Picnic tables can be placed outside the clear zone and have to meet current Americans with Disabilities Act requirements. The guidelines do not allow the placement of emergency parking signs at pull-off areas with picnic tables.

The signs used at the picnic areas and FSPs are in accordance with the *Manual on Uniform Traffic Control Devices* (MUTCD),[36] Section 2D-42, "Rest Area Signs." Unlike the picnic and emergency parking pull-off areas, the FSPs have deceleration and acceleration ramps. The Commission uses emergency parking signs that are similar to those prescribed in the MUTCD, Section 2B-34, "Emergency Parking Signs." The MUTCD states that these signs are to be horizontal rectangles with a black legend on a white background and recommends that the size of signs on freeways be 4 by 3 feet. During nighttime testing by the Safety Board, these signs were clearly visible to approaching traffic.

The Commission does not define what constitutes an emergency for vehicles parked in the emergency parking or any pull-off area, nor does it regulate traffic using the pull-off areas that are not marked. The Commission contends that, if a driver is fatigued or if a commercial driver needs to stop to avoid hours-of-service violations, the emergency parking and other pull-off areas provide a zone where a stopped vehicle can be off and away from the travel lanes of the turnpike. The Commission discourages the use of shoulders other than during a mechanical break down and encourages the removal of a vehicle as quickly as possible. The Commission believes a vehicle on the shoulder poses a greater risk to other vehicles because of its proximity to the roadway.

---

[35] *Guidelines for Signing Pull-Off Areas as Emergency Parking Areas* and *Guidelines for Placement of Picnic Tables in Pull-Off Areas.*

[36] U.S. Department of Transportation Federal Highway Administration, *Manual on Uniform Traffic Control Devices, For Streets and Highways*, 1988 edition.

Truck Parking Facilities

A few days after the accident, during its on-scene investigation, the Safety Board surveyed the pull-off areas, east and westbound, between the accident site (MP 184.9) and interchange 12 (MP 161.4), and observed their use for truck parking. (See table 4.)

Table 4. Pull-off area utilization.

Direction	Milepost	A.M.	Vehicles	Notes
Westbound	*185.0	2:57	4 Combinations	3 Illuminated with marker lights
	*183.3	2:59	None	
	*181.1	3:01	None	
	178.8	3:04	None	
	178.4	3:07	None	3 White/orange stripe vertical barriers
	177.8	3:11	None	Left-hand curve
	176.7	3:14	None	
Eastbound	173.8	4:07	9 Combinations	4 Illuminated with marker lights
	174.5	4:09	1 Combination	No lights on
	175.2	4:11	None	
	176.4	4:12	None	Closed and barricaded
	176.7	4:14	1 Combination	No lights on 3 reflective triangles
	*179.2	4:19	3 Combinations	3 Illuminated with marker lights
	*183.8	4:24	**3 Combinations 1 Passenger car	2 Illuminated with marker lights no lights on car
	*184.7	4:26	7 Combinations	6 Illuminated with marker lights

* Des gnated as emergency park ng area

** One comb nat on rece v ng ass stance from mob e repa r truck

Table 5 provides information on the signage of pull-off areas throughout the turnpike, as observed by Safety Board investigators.

Commercial Vehicle Parking Space. The U.S. Department of Transportation (DOT) contracted with the Trucking Research Institute (TRI)[37] in 1992 to study the adequacy of truck parking at public rest areas along the interstate system. The results of the study,[38] published by the American Trucking Associations, Inc., (ATA) in 1996, found a shortfall of 28,400 truck parking spaces in rest areas nationwide. It stated:

---

[37] TRI is the research component of the American Trucking Associations Foundation, Inc., an affiliate of the ATA.

[38] *Commercial Driver Rest Area Requirements: No Room at the Inn*, American Trucking Association Foundation, Inc., 1996, ATA Product Code: C0887.

The average current national truck parking space shortfall per rest area is 21. On a rest area basis, this shortfall is the highest in Connecticut, New Jersey, South Carolina, and Tennessee. . . . States where the current shortfall estimates are greatest include California, Pennsylvania, New York, Texas, and Virginia.

Table 5. Pennsylvania Turnpike pull-off areas.

Turnpike Area	Signed Emergency Parking	Unmarked	Signed No Parking
Eastbound From Pittsburgh (exit 6) To New Jersey border	35	156	9
Westbound From New Jersey border To Pittsburgh (exit 6)	38	*130	4
North/Southbound Northeast Extension	8	64	**9
Westbound From Pittsburgh (exit 6) To Ohio border	18	74	2
Eastbound From Ohio border To Pittsburgh (exit 6)	5	31	0

* Severa of the unmarked pu -off areas d sp ayed p cn c area s gns
** No park ng s gns were ocated near emergency ca boxes

The TRI study found a total of 63 rest areas in Pennsylvania. (The turnpike's 22 FSPs comprised 35 percent of that total.) In the 63 rest areas, approximately 1,175 truck parking spaces were available, and the study indicated a need for about 3,157 spaces, implying a shortfall of about 1,982 truck parking spaces. Based on the model used in this study, Pennsylvania had the highest truck parking space shortfall.

The TRI study proposed that additional truck parking spaces be based on the relationship between accident rates and parking shortfall estimates and suggested that a shortfall in truck parking spaces may contribute to accidents.

In addition, the TRI study determined that truck pull-off areas may be appropriate in rural areas with great distances between rest areas and as a short-term solution to solve the nationwide shortfall of truck parking spaces. It stated that

> truck pull-off areas offer benefits of supplying additional parking for trucks without the cost of a full-service rest area and satisfies the needs of truck drivers to have quiet, accessible, and convenient stopping places for short-term rest along the interstates. The Pennsylvania Turnpike makes the most successful use of truck pull-off areas which are adjacent to and visible from the interstate.

Between August 31 and September 2, 1999, the Safety Board held a public hearing in Nashville on Advanced Safety Technology Applications for Commercial Vehicles at which the president of the ATA further stressed the need for additional rest areas for commercial vehicles. He reminded the Safety Board that the shortfalls stated in the TRI study were based on 1992 data. He added that the study had a projected shortfall for 1997 of 35,000 spaces along the interstate, based on a model that used a conservative growth rate of about 1 percent for truck demand. According to the ATA president, actual trucking demands for spaces have far exceeded the growth projections of the TRI study and are expected to grow more than 30 percent between 1997 and 2007.

Transportation Equity Act for the 21st Century. The TEA 21, enacted on June 9, 1998, requires that the U.S. Secretary of Transportation determine the location and quantity of parking facilities at commercial truck stops, travel plazas, and public rest areas that can be used by motor carriers to comply with Federal hours-of-service rules. Section 4027 of TEA 21 calls for (1) a nationwide inventory of rest areas and other parking facilities along the national highway system; (2) an analysis of shortages, real and projected; and (3) the development of a plan to reduce the shortages. These initiatives are to be delivered to the U.S. Congress by June 2001. Section 4027 further stipulates that this research is to be conducted in cooperation with research organizations that represent the motor carrier industry, the travel plaza industry, and commercial motor vehicle drivers.

On June 29 and 30, 1999, the OMCHS hosted a rest area forum for State enforcement and department of transportation officials, motor carriers, private truck stop operators, commercial drivers, safety advocates, and other interested parties. The OMCHS intends to use the results of the forum to help formulate the research proposal to fulfill the requirements of section 4027.

Pathological and Toxicological Information

On June 21, 1998, three full and four limited postmortem examinations were performed on the accident fatalities (the busdriver and six passengers). According to the pathology findings, the injuries sustained by all seven were the result of multiple blunt trauma.

The Civil Aeromedical Institute in Oklahoma City, Oklahoma, conducted toxicological testing of the busdriver's blood and bodily fluids obtained during the postmortem examination. The report was negative for the presence of alcohol and specified illegal drugs.[39] It noted that diphenhydramine (an antihistamine, commonly known by the trade name Benadryl);[40] pseudoephedrine (a decongestant, commonly known by the trade name Sudafed); phenylpropanolamine (a decongestant and metabolite of pseudoephedrine); and acetaminophen (commonly known by the trade name Tylenol) were detected. The concentration of these substances was found to be as follows:

---

[39] Marijuana, cocaine, phencylidine (PCP), opiates, and amphetamines.

[40] The over-the-counter medication includes a warning label about using caution when driving a motor vehicle or operating machinery.

diphenhydramine – 0.073 ug/ml in blood and 0.257 ug/ml in liver fluid.

pseudoephedrine – detected in blood and liver fluid but no concentration given.

phenylpropanolamine – detected in blood and liver fluid but no concentration given.

acetaminophen – 12 ug/ml in blood.

Greyhound policy requires employees to notify the company about their use of prescription drugs and over-the-counter medication that could adversely affect their ability to safely perform their job. This policy states that employees who perform work that could endanger Greyhound personnel or the public are obligated to advise Greyhound of their use of this type of medication and to refrain from performing such work. No Federal regulation governs the use of nonprescription medication by commercial drivers.

Title 49 CFR 382.213 states:

> No driver shall report for duty or remain on duty requiring the performance of safety sensitive functions when the driver uses any controlled substance, except when the use is pursuant to the instructions of a licensed medical practitioner, as defined in Sec. 382.107 of this part, who has advised the driver that the substance will not adversely affect the driver's ability to safely operate a commercial motor vehicle.

Greyhound contracted with a forensic pathologist and then with a clinical pathologist to review microscopic slides of cardiac material prepared during the busdriver's autopsy. In a May 6, 1999, letter to an attorney representing Greyhound, the forensic pathologist stated that

> the lacerated aorta and the tear in the right ventricular wall . . . are . . . of traumatic origin and occurred at the time of the impact. . . . Another section depicts a focal area of intermural hemorrhage, that is bleeding within the vessel wall of the coronary artery, which is not geographically located where trauma occurred to the heart. . . . A hemorrhage of this type reducing the available blood flow can be expected to produce anginal pain and eventually myocardial infarction.

In a July 15, 1999, letter to the same attorney, the clinical pathologist, after reviewing the forensic pathologist's report, noted that the busdriver

> clearly . . . died from massive trauma sustained in the accident. . . . the microscopic examination of the coronary arteries . . . . shows clear evidence of hemorrhagic dissection. . . . It is highly unlikely that the hemorrhage reflected trauma. . . . The most likely scenario in this case was 1) hemorrhage into a coronary plaque, 2) acute myocardial infarction, 3) sudden cardiac arrhythmia and 4) failure of the circulation and loss of consciousness.

An independent review of all retained cardiac material from the autopsy by forensic pathologists at the Armed Forces Institute of Pathology (AFIP) in October 1999 confirmed the presence of bleeding in the coronary artery wall but concluded that "in the absence of documented signs or symptoms of myocardial ischemia[41] just prior to the collision, this autopsy finding cannot be used to determine the role of the coronary artery disease in the mishap [footnote added]."

Survival Aspects

One passenger, who is a physician, stated that she was sitting alone on the right side of the bus in the fifth or sixth row from the front. She was resting her head between the window and the seatback, attempting to sleep. She said that, when the accident occurred, she was thrown "very forcefully" into the seat in front of her, hit her head on the seat and window, and fell to the left onto the floor. She then was pinned between the aisle floor and aisle seat because another passenger had fallen on top of her.

This passenger stated that visibility inside the bus was very poor because of the dust from the accident and the lack of lights. She said that, after the accident, the bus was "pitch black" and very quiet. She called out for everyone who was able to move to evacuate the bus because she could smell gasoline fumes. She stated that, at one point when they were attempting to evacuate the bus, another passenger ignited a cigarette lighter to provide lighting and she instructed him to quickly extinguish it because of the gasoline fumes and her fear of a fire.

She was not familiar with the emergency exits before the accident, and another passenger opened an emergency window on the left side of the bus through which she exited. She stated that she encountered difficulties escaping the bus because it was a "very long jump, and [she] could use only one arm to evacuate." She scraped the front of her body against the side of the bus and injured herself further while escaping.

This passenger stated that the emergency personnel arrived after "probably about 30 to 40 minutes." She recalled having difficulty in awaking the truckdrivers parked near the accident to ask them to call for help. The first emergency responders she observed were paramedics and then firefighters, who were triaging and assisting passengers.

A second passenger on board the accident bus recalled that he was asleep on the left side bench seat across from the restroom when the accident occurred and did not remember the collision. He said that he was thrown about two or three seats forward by the impact. He then opened the left side emergency exit window near where he landed and let other passengers out. He stated that he knew how to open the window because during the journey he had read the instructions posted on the emergency exit handle.

A third passenger reported that, when evacuating the bus, everyone used the same emergency exit window to escape. He stated that he did not understand why the other windows did not automatically open when the accident occurred; he did not know about the emergency roof hatches. He said that the passengers could not see the emergency exits

---

[41] Ischemia refers to localized reduction in blood supply due to obstruction of inflow of arterial blood (as by the narrowing of arteries by spasm or disease).

because of the darkness. He also said that he had been riding Greyhound buses for many years, yet was not aware of the emergency signage indicating the exit locations and instructions on how to use them in an emergency.

Another passenger told Safety Board investigators that he was seated alone on the right side of the bus in row eight or nine next to the window. He was sleeping fully reclined in his seat with his head toward the window before the accident and recalled falling to the left and forward, striking his head on the aisle seat handle during the accident sequence, and being pulled out of his seat by an emergency responder. He was the last passenger to exit the bus and was helped by emergency responders to go out a window and down a ladder. He stated that he was able to see inside the bus because by the time he exited the bus, the emergency responders were inside cutting the seats of trapped passengers.

When the emergency responders arrived, they set up a step ladder (see figure 9), which the other Greyhound busdriver who had stopped at the accident scene used to climb into the bus and open the emergency windows. He then showed the responders how to use the extrication tools to remove the windows to gain access to the bus to reach the injured. He stated that he had trouble with visibility inside the bus because "it was pitch black and you couldn't see." The IC said that had the other Greyhound busdriver not been present to point out where the exits were, the lack of markings on the outside of the bus to indicate the exits would have been a hindrance.

Figure 9. Outside left side of accident bus with emergency responders.

Another firefighter reported that he did not remember whether he observed any lights on the bus because the firefighters immediately set up the truck generator to provide additional lighting at the scene. He added that, had the generator not been available for lighting, the responders had flashlights for use inside the bus.

Emergency Management

Hustontown (Fulton County) Volunteer Fire and Rescue Company

After the EMT who received the initial 911 call had dispatched Hustontown, he responded to the accident scene in an ambulance. He stated that he had no communication with the IC, but contacted the rescue captain when he arrived on scene to inquire where his services were needed. According to the EMT, he had had previous experience that involved a charter bus accident several years earlier; he expressed a concern about a need for more training in operations to improve the turnpike emergency response.

After the accident, a Safety Board investigator interviewed two other Hustontown technicians, identified as EMT-2 and EMT-3. They recalled that they were notified at their residence about 4:30 a.m. and left together for the accident scene in their personal vehicle. They arrived on scene between 4:40 and 4:45 a.m. The Hustontown assistant chief was already on scene and had called them while they were en route to report what was happening at the accident site. They said that, after arriving on scene, they did not call in at any time through the dispatch radio because they had no dispatcher. They employed the 4606 radio frequency.

They said that, after they arrived, they started triage on the 10 to 15 "walking wounded" from the bus because it appeared enough responders were inside the bus. As more responders arrived and assisted with triage, EMT-2 started coordinating which ambulances would take which patients and in which order. He stated that he found no one was handling this activity and he took charge. He had one patient experiencing chest pains transported first. He also had ambulances stand by for the injured remaining on the bus and placed specific patients into the ambulances. EMT-2 said that he was contacting the hospitals to alert them of the patients that would be arriving.

According to EMT-2, he had never been involved in a response to an accident such as this one. He had experience in a response to a two-car accident in May 1998 involving eight injuries, but no fatalities. He said that his fire company carries out training drills and, "once in a while," two companies coordinate joint training. EMT-2 was an Emergency Management Agency (EMA) coordinate for Hustontown. He stated that the township had a county disaster emergency management plan, which was very vague. He recalled that at first, while on scene, he did not even think about the EMA until after more responders had arrived and enough manpower was present. Neither EMT-2 nor EMT-3 had participated in a local mass casualty drill for at least 12 years; both had been with the Hustontown company for the last 2 years.

Metal Township (Franklin County) Fire and Rescue Company

Metal Township initially dispatched one ambulance and one fire truck with six firefighters. Of the six firefighters, three were EMTs. The ambulance was a basic life support ambulance, and the first arriving triage officer was an EMT from the ambulance. The Hustontown assistant chief, who was already on scene, was assigned triage responsibilities for the passengers who had evacuated the bus. The victims inside the bus were separately triaged.

According to the Metal Township fire chief (the IC for the accident), when Metal Township responds to an accident on the turnpike, the incident is essentially under the turnpike's emergency management system. The first arriving unit to respond is responsible for assessing the scene and the number and type of injuries and for requesting as many units and as much equipment as needed. He said that, after arriving on scene, he assessed the situation and then requested the resources and equipment he needed, including additional ambulances and helicopters.

The IC stated that he directed communications to move the fire and rescue operations to channel 2 (Franklin County's second fire ground channel) to keep the continuous fire and rescue communications off the main dispatch channel. He added that communications were a problem because in Franklin County the medical and fire ground channels were different. The medical channel was on a high band frequency, which the ambulances used; the fire ground channel was on a low band frequency, which was in his vehicle and used on scene. Furthermore, the other counties had a different frequency. So, he observed, responders needed three or four different radios to communicate. He stated that he did not have those radios available and a communication lapse occurred, preventing him from communicating with everyone on scene. In addition, because information was being sent on the medical channel and the IC had a low band channel for the fire company activities, he said that he was not aware that the Fulton County Medical Center could not receive any more patients and patients had to be sent to the Chambersburg Hospital. He recalled asking the Metal Township EMT captain to track the ambulances' destinations and the class of patient being transported.

The IC also expressed several concerns about the emergency response. He remarked that it "wasn't an organized thing. It was a pretty seat-of-the-pants type deal. We'd never dealt with anything like this before." When asked whether the situation was chaotic, the IC replied, "yes." Most emergency response call needs in the past, according to the IC, were not of the magnitude of this accident; multiple-car accidents occur but usually not with this number of fatalities. He said that under the box card assignment set up for turnpike accidents, a prearranged number of units are dispatched to a specific accident, a prearranged number for every situation. The box card assignment set up for this accident provided for a dispatch of four ambulances and one rescue vehicle. He believed that sufficient emergency response resources should be available at dispatch for this type of accident; when he arrived on scene and assessed the situation, he found that he did not have the resources present initially to cope with such an accident.

The IC stated that he had no bus rescue training before the accident and that the emergency responders would benefit from training on commercial buses. He said that Franklin County does perform countywide disaster drills[42] and had one a few months before the accident, although Metal Township did not attend because the drill was held on the other side of the county. The IC also noted that turnpike safety personnel hold a group meeting with the responders once a year, but he thought that no one is obliged to attend.

Cumberland Valley (Cumberland County) Hose Company

Safety Board investigators interviewed a Cumberland Valley paramedic/EMT, who arrived on scene about 4:30 a.m. His first task was to determine whether several of the passengers in the bus were deceased. He found that six people were dead and one was still alive and then left the bus to allow the rescue units to cut out the seats that were entrapping the bodies.

According to the paramedic, throughout the incident, he did not know the identity of the IC and did not learn his identity until the accident debriefing, which occurred several days later. He stated that he had asked who was the IC and reported that "no one really knew." He recalled, "it was total, pretty much chaos" and noted that responders generally did what they wanted to and that no one was directing the ambulances to the hospitals. He advised that an emergency medical services (EMS) commander, a rescue commander, and a fire commander should have been present, as well as someone staging all the arriving units. He said that when he tried to radio the command post to obtain orders, no one answered when he called, "command post, command post."

West End (Cumberland County) Fire and Rescue

The West End Fire and Rescue Department in Shippensburg, Pennsylvania, was called to respond in the second dispatch at 4:43 a.m. The department is about 25 to 30 miles and about 32 minutes from the accident scene and has between 40 and 50 volunteer firefighters. According to department officials, West End was the appropriate heavy rescue fire department to have been called with the vehicles involved in this accident.

The West End chief and deputy chief told Safety Board investigators that, while en route to the accident scene, the communications dispatcher identified the IC and advised them to switch to radio channel 2 for all fire and rescue activities. At this time, radio channel Franklin 1 was the dispatcher; channel 2 was the fire and rescue operations channel; and medic 10 was the medical channel. After arriving on scene, they had contact with the IC several times. The IC assigned their team to extricate the trapped passengers remaining in the bus because the initial responders were tiring.

The chief and deputy chief expressed some concerns about the response. When notification was initially received that the accident involved a bus and a tractor-semitrailer, West End, as the heavy duty response unit, should have immediately been

---

[42] Franklin County has an emergency management coordinator who maintains the records of the disaster drills held.

dispatched, especially since it has the same dispatcher. According to the chief and deputy chief, an immediate dispatch would have saved about 15 minutes, which can be important to a response. Instead, dispatch occurred after the IC arrived on scene and called for mutual aid, and the equipment was 32 minutes from the scene. In the county where West End normally operates, its box card assignment for mass casualties always includes at least two heavy duty squads, two full engine companies, four basic life support ambulances, and perhaps one or two medic units, with a helicopter on standby. They explained that, based on the dispatch description of this accident, additional units should have been requested immediately and then sent to a staging area away from the accident scene. These resources could then have been requested and received without delay had a need existed, resulting in less chaos and confusion.

West End had participated in mass casualty drills within the county, but not in any turnpike drills. The chief and deputy chief said that they had trained on school buses but had never had a drill with a motorcoach. The last drill that they had participated in took place 6 months before the accident and involved an explosion at a dormitory. The Franklin County companies and EMS and the Cumberland County EMS had also participated.

Turnpike Incident Management Program and Command System

The Commission has published an *Incident Management Program Book* and *Incident Command System Manual*. These publications, from which the following information was obtained, describe the functions of the incident management program and command system.

Incident Management

In September 1988, the Commission formed its incident management team, which is composed of PSP and turnpike operations personnel. The team of about 30 members meets regularly and reviews incidents that have occurred on the turnpike. After the team review, the Commission then implements measures to improve incident management. Committees are formed to develop and implement initiatives and report findings to the team for disposition. The Contracted Services Committee is responsible for fire services, and the Joint Panel for Ambulance Services manages the EMS companies.

The Commission's various subcommittees for emergency services are responsible for holding annual informational meetings, which are conducted across the State for volunteer emergency service groups and county dispatch centers. According to the Commission, State police and turnpike personnel are available at the meetings to discuss accident and safety procedures and any operational or protocol problems. In addition to the meetings, the Commission has committee member contacts available for the emergency services at all times to notify them of problems, concerns, or suggestions.

Communications Center

The Commission maintains its Operations Control Center (communications center) in Highspire, operating 24 hours a day 365 days a year. Incidents are reported to the communications center through different sources, including call boxes, CB radios, turnpike personnel, *11 cellular calls, and State police maintenance. The center receives an average of 1,300 call box calls every month and 400 calls and 1,400 radio transmissions daily. It is equipped with a CAD (computer-aided dispatch) system, which is designed to provide the radio operators with instantaneous access to the closest emergency services and State police for any incident at any location on the turnpike. The communications center controls the radio communications for turnpike personnel, customers, State police, authorized services, and emergency fire and ambulance services. It dispatches the appropriate personnel, such as State police, fire and ambulance services, emergency spill response, medical helicopters, and specialized equipment.

Emergency Response Services

According to the Commission, it is the only highway agency in the State that contracts with fire and medical service providers for emergency service on the roadway. The contracts, according to the Commission, are established to provide a means of compensation for the volunteer fire and emergency medical services in Pennsylvania and to improve the quality of emergency service available. The Commission contracts 82 fire companies and 65 EMS providers and assigns each to a specific coverage area.

The Commission provides radios to the contracted fire services and EMS providers that do not have radios compatible with the turnpike's communication system. When an incident occurs, according to the Commission, all responding State police, turnpike units, and emergency services are capable of communicating with each other during their response. To improve communications at the scene, hand-held portable radios with repeaters are used in State police and turnpike units.

A dual dispatch system, under which emergency units are dispatched in both directions, is employed on the turnpike for emergency, fire, rescue, and EMS providers responding in selected areas: where traffic is heavy, where the distance is unusually long between interchanges or crossovers, and where the exact location or direction of an incident has not been confirmed. The first directional company to locate the incident deals with it, and the other units return to their station. According to the Commission, dual dispatch has successfully improved response times to incidents.

In addition, to enhance the response efforts of the contracted emergency services, emergency access gates are located throughout the turnpike system; many of the access locations were recommended by the emergency services themselves as a measure to improve their response efforts.

Pennsylvania State Police Troop T

The Commission-funded Troop T of the PSP is assigned to control traffic and enforce all State laws on the turnpike. Troop T officers have the ultimate authority at all incidents on the turnpike and oversee all responding agencies. Troop T is assisted by the turnpike's 20-facility maintenance department, which is equipped with first responder vehicles. One location also provides ambulance service. Emergency response workers are scheduled 24 hours a day and are all trained in CPR, advanced first aid, and hazardous materials recognition and identification; some of the emergency response workers are certified EMTs. They are responsible for attending injured patients until outside medical assistance arrives.

The standard first responder vans are equipped with cellular phones, CB radios, turnpike repeaters, and portable radios for communications. The vans carry emergency medical supplies, incident command kits, and spill containment materials. Five customized emergency response vehicles are also available, especially for use in hazardous materials spills and as command posts.

The PSP indicated that, when an incident occurs within the turnpike system, the maintenance department sets up a mobile command post that is used to coordinate organization and communication. In any incident on the turnpike, the highest ranking PSP officer at the scene is in charge and acts as the turnpike IC. The PSP and the maintenance department are responsible for clearing accident scenes according to the following priorities: life safety, incident stabilization, and traffic flow restoration. The on-scene maintenance supervisor, in cooperation with the PSP, has the authority to take any action reasonably necessary to ensure customer safety and to promptly clear the roadway.

Incident Command System

The Commission has adopted the Incident Command System (ICS) as its structure to manage all incidents that occur within the turnpike system. Goals of the ICS include achieving better communication and coordination at the scene among fire and rescue, ambulance, authorized service, PSP, turnpike maintenance personnel, and other agencies; improving overall safety at the scene by providing immediate medical care, when needed; managing traffic efficiently; clearing accident scenes expeditiously; and shortening periods of road closures. Turnpike representatives and the PSP assigned to the turnpike have jointly attended a 16-hour ICS training program.

The Commission provides key operational ICS personnel (the State police and maintenance, fire, rescue, and EMS command staff) with incident command field kits, which include command staff vests, as well as blank check-in sheets and structure organizational forms to assist in documentation. The ICS eliminates the 10-code radio system and uses clear text, or plain English, for all radio transmissions to reduce the likelihood of miscommunications at accident scenes.

The *Incident Command System Manual* is sectioned into five modules: the introduction and overview, the ICS command and command staff, the general staff functions and applications, the incident management policies and procedures, and several accident scenarios that would require establishment of the ICS. Included in the scenarios is one in which a Greyhound bus has run off the road and down an embankment with a fatality and minor and serious injuries. The accident depicted in the scenario occurred in

Donegal, Pennsylvania, on June 26, 1991, and was investigated by the Safety Board.[43] The scenario indicates potential problems that may be encountered and lists emergency response units and apparatus that may be required. According to the Commission, the manual is provided to the contracted fire and medical departments.

Postaccident Tests

The motorcoach's power steering hydraulic pump was removed by Safety Board investigators for examination and functional testing, which was performed at the manufacturer's facility. Test results showed the pump to be operating within the manufacturer's production specifications for new pumps and performing as well as a new unit at the time of the accident.

The Safety Board's Materials Laboratory conducted a forensic examination of the speedometer assembly and 22 lamp assemblies and bulbs for the presence of "needle slap"[44] and "hot stretch,"[45] respectively. The examination revealed no evidence of needle slap; the headlight assembly and several of the submitted bulbs exhibited evidence of stretching. (See appendix B for TransAm tractor-semitrailer test information.)

Additionally, the Safety Board conducted deceleration tests, using a bus similar to the accident bus, on the paved shoulder near the accident site with the surface both dry and wet. A VeriCom-2000 accelerometer/decelerometer was mounted on the aisle of the bus approximately 6 feet behind the steps to measure the deceleration rates. See table 6 for the data collected.

Table 6. Deceleration testing data.

Surface Condition	Speed mph	Time Seconds	Distance Feet	Peak Deceleration	Average Deceleration
Dry	31.1	2.63	--	19.2 ft/sec	17.1 ft/sec
Wet	32.5	2.87	68	19.0 ft/sec	16.4 ft/sec

---

[43] National Transportation Safety Board. 1992. *Greyhound Run-off-the-Road Accidents, Donegal, Pennsylvania, June 26, 1991, and Caroline, New York, August 3, 1991.* Highway Accident Report NTSB/HAR-92/01. Washington, DC.

[44] A condition in which the speedometer needle comes in contact with the face of the speedometer when subjected to impact.

[45] A condition that results when a filament is illuminated and subjected to impact.

Analysis

Exclusions

The east and westbound traffic lanes were separated by 45-inch-tall Jersey barriers. The pull-off area began beyond the uphill grade and was designated with signs approaching it. Pavement markings were visible and in good condition. According to witnesses, it was not raining.

Postaccident mechanical inspections of the bus, including the coach's brake actuators, foundation brakes, and steering components, revealed no defects or deficiencies. Based on the statement by the State trooper who observed the bus immediately before the accident, speeding was not involved. The busdriver's postaccident toxicological tests were negative for alcohol and illicit drugs.

The Safety Board therefore concludes that neither the existing highway pavement conditions, the mechanical condition of the bus, nor the weather contributed to the accident. The busdriver did not appear to be speeding, nor was he impaired by alcohol or illicit drugs.

The remainder of this analysis will address the safety issues that were raised by this accident, including the busdriver's performance, the adequacy of carrier oversight, the adequacy of the design and the appropriateness of the use of pull-off areas, the lack of motorcoach emergency interior lighting and retroreflective signage, and the organization of the disaster preparedness and emergency response management.

The Accident

Busdriver Performance

The Safety Board's investigation found several factors that support the position that the busdriver had trouble staying awake around the time of the accident. These factors include the busdriver's irregular driving schedule, eyewitness' accounts, and postaccident evidence. The Safety Board also examined the possibility that a medical condition impaired the busdriver and that his use of an over-the-counter antihistamine contributed to his drowsiness.

Medical. Although the Greyhound medical records[46] indicated that the accident busdriver used medication for high blood pressure from 1993 to 1995, his personal medical records indicated normal blood pressure and no prescribed medications between

---

[46] Medical records are retained by Greyhound for only 5 years.

1996 and 1998. In November 1997, during a visit to his family physician, the busdriver noted that he sometimes drove 18 hours per day, and he complained of short-term memory loss, irritability, insomnia, and a nonradiating left-sided chest pain when at rest. A subsequent examination that included an electrocardiogram, blood work, and a Thallium stress test found only slightly elevated cholesterol levels. The stress test was interpreted as unremarkable, with "no evidence of stress-induced ischemia."

The busdriver's autopsy report concluded that his death was caused by the multiple injuries he sustained from the accident; the toxicology evaluation did not reveal the presence of any heart or blood pressure medications. The forensic pathologist and the clinical pathologist, contracted by Greyhound to review slides of cardiac material prepared during the autopsy, noted a single slide with an area of bleeding that the forensic pathologist attributed to a nontraumatic event preceding the accident, a judgement with which the clinical pathologist agreed. On the basis of this finding, one of the pathologists concluded that the driver was distracted by chest pain, and the other concluded that the driver suffered loss-of-consciousness immediately before the accident. The independent review of cardiac material by forensic pathologists at the AFIP confirmed the presence of bleeding in the coronary artery wall but concluded that "in the absence of documented signs or symptoms of myocardial ischemia just prior to the collision, this autopsy finding cannot be used to determine the role of the coronary artery disease in the mishap." The Safety Board concludes that the evidence cannot establish that the busdriver was impaired or incapacitated by a cardiac condition prior to the accident.

The postaccident toxicological blood tests performed on the Greyhound driver found the presence of the decongestants pseudoephedrine, commonly known by the trade name Sudafed™, and phenylpropanolamine, a metabolite of pseudoephedrine. Pseudoephedrine is often used in combination with an antihistamine in over-the-counter and prescription preparations for multisymptom cold and allergy relief. It may act as a mild stimulant and is not likely to have any significant detrimental effect on performance. Also present in the driver's blood was acetaminophen, the over-the-counter painkiller and fever-reducer found in Tylenol™, which is frequently used in multisymptom cold and allergy preparations in combination with an antihistamine or a decongestant or both. The level detected is therapeutic and suggests relatively recent ingestion of a normal dose of the medication, which is not likely to have any significant detrimental effect on performance.

The toxicological tests also revealed the presence of diphenhydramine, a sedating antihistamine commonly known by the trade name Benadryl™, in the accident driver's blood. Diphenhydramine is used in cold and allergy preparations and in sleep aids. In therapeutic doses, the medication commonly results in drowsiness and has measurable effects on complex cognitive and motor tasks, such as driving a vehicle. The levels of antihistamine detected in his blood were therapeutic and consistent with at least a normal, single dose ingested within the previous few hours. Therefore, the Safety Board concludes that the busdriver ingested an over-the-counter multisymptom cold and allergy medication at some time either shortly before or during his scheduled route. The sedating antihistamine in this medication contributed to making the busdriver sleepy and reducing his alertness.

Note: The Safety Board is currently investigating the issue of over-the-counter medication and its effect on transportation safety across all modes.

Driver's Work Schedule. The schedule selected by the busdriver resulted in an irregular work-rest cycle. The busdriver's on-duty time commenced anywhere between 9:00 p.m. and 1:30 a.m., and his off-duty time began anywhere between 9:00 a.m. and 12:30 p.m. (See figure 10.) The Safety Board has previously addressed the issue of operator fatigue involving irregular work-rest schedules in its 1995 safety study on heavy truck accidents.[47] In the subset of these accidents for which sleep data were available, the Safety Board found about 67 percent of the drivers (43 of 64) with irregular schedules were involved in fatigue-related accidents, compared with about 38 percent of drivers (9 of 24) with regular schedules. The Safety Board found that irregular schedules could result in more hours awake than normal and, without careful planning, prevent drivers from obtaining adequate sleep.

Time Schedule

DAY OF THE WEEK	TIME SCHEDULE	TOUR ACTIVITY
Shift #1 (June 17)		Pittsburgh, PA, to New York, NY
Shift #2 (June 18)		New York, NY, to Pittsburgh, PA
Shift #3 (June 18-19)		Pittsburgh, PA, to New York, NY
Shift #4 (June 19-20)		New York, NY, to Burnt Cabins, PA

On Duty

Uncertain

Night

6PM 9PM 12AM 3AM 6AM 9AM 12PM 3PM 6PM

Figure 10. Chart of shift schedule.

The busdriver was in the 4th day of a 4-day schedule, during which he slept in the daylight hours and drove in the nighttime hours, contrary to his usual off-day routine. Research has shown that nightshift work schedules are generally more tiring for workers than dayshift work schedules, with nightshift workers usually getting less uninterrupted

---

[47] A driver's work-rest hours are classified as irregular if the start times of two consecutive duty periods and the start times of two consecutive sleep periods both vary by 2 or more hours at least twice during a 96-hour period. See National Transportation Safety Board. 1995. *Factors that Affect Fatigue in Heavy Truck Accidents.* Safety Study Report NTSB/SS-95/01. Washington, DC.

sleep per day.[48] In addition, the accident occurred at approximately 4:05 a.m., the time of day when a driver would be most likely to experience sleepiness and a loss of alertness due to the body's circadian rhythm.[49]

The busdriver had previously been observed to have difficulty staying awake during nighttime driving. Six months before the accident, a passenger witnessed episodes of drowsiness on the part of the driver during which he repeatedly drifted off the roadway, was alerted by contact with rumble strips, and then steered back onto the roadway. In addition, shortly before the accident occurred, an off-duty State trooper observed a Greyhound bus drifting onto the right shoulder and returning to the roadway about 0.5 mile from the accident site, suggesting that this bus was the one driven by the driver in this accident.

The motorcoach departed the roadway at an angle of approximately 3 degrees. The shallowness of the angle suggests that the vehicle drifted from the roadway as the driver was falling asleep.[50] The 28-foot tire marks discovered at the scene of the accident by Safety Board investigators, matching the departure angle of the bus, were included in a computer simulation of the accident. The results of this simulation supported the judgement that the marks originated from the accident bus. These marks suggest that the driver did not react quickly enough to apply the brakes until it was too late to avoid the collision.

A forensic examination of the taillights of the TransAm semitrailer indicated that they were illuminated at the time of impact, which, in conjunction with the red and white retroreflective conspicuity sheeting (see appendix B), suggests that the rear of the parked TransAm truck should have been clearly visible at night to approaching westbound drivers. An FHWA study[51] conducted in the late 1970s determined that fatigued drivers would follow the markings and lights of trucks parked on a roadway shoulder, referred to as the "moth to the light effect." The TransAm truck was parked about 9 feet from the travel lane, and its lights may have acted as a potential beacon to the accident busdriver. However, it should be noted that although the moth to the light effect is frequently an explanation for accidents of this type among many in the regulatory and law enforcement community, there is currently little evidence supporting this phenomenon.[52]

Furthermore, the busdriver had complained to his physician in November 1997 about difficulty sleeping, stating that he was able to sleep only 3 to 4 hours before waking.

---

[48] McDonald, N., *Fatigue, Safety and the Truck Driver*. Long: Taylor and Francis. 1984.

[49] Circadian rhythm describes the regular recurrence, in cycles of about 24 hours, of biological processes or activities, such as sensitivity to drugs and stimuli, hormone secretion, sleeping, and feeding. This rhythm seems to set by a "biological clock" that appears to be set by recurring daylight and darkness. Also see Rosekind, M.R., *Fatigue in Transportation: Physiological, Performance, and Safety Issues*. Prepared for the National Transportation Safety Board. Washington, DC. April 1999.

[50] Knipling, R.R., and Wang, J.S., "Crashes and Fatalities Related to Driver Drowsiness/Fatigue." *Research Note*. November 1994. National Highway Traffic Safety Administration. Washington, DC.

[51] *Commercial Vehicles in Collisions Involving Vehicles Parked or Stopped on Highway Shoulders*, U.S. Department of Transportation, Federal Highway Administration, and Bureau of Motor Carrier Safety, June 16, 1977.

This suggests that the driver might have accumulated a substantial sleep debt by the 4th day of his shift, resulting in a highly fatigued state.[53] Insomnia may have contributed to his fatigue; research shows that "the more sleep is disturbed or reduced for whatever reason, the more likely an individual will inadvertently slip into sleep."[54] Losing as little as 2 hours of sleep can negatively affect alertness and performance, leading to degraded judgment, decisionmaking, and memory; slowed reaction time; lack of concentration; fixation; and irritability.[55]

The Safety Board concludes that because of the scheduled irregular work-rest cycle and possible sleeping difficulties, the busdriver may have developed a sleep debt over the 4 days of his shift, which was exacerbated by a reduced alertness corresponding to his body's circadian rhythm. The combined result of these factors may have contributed to the busdriver's sleepiness and reduced alertness, causing him to drift off the roadway and collide with the tractor-semitrailer parked in the adjacent emergency parking area. Therefore, the Safety Board believes that Greyhound should revise driver scheduling practices to reduce scheduling variability that results in irregular work-rest cycles. In addition, the Safety Board believes that the United Motorcoach Association (UMA) and the American Bus Association (ABA) should advise their members of the facts and circumstances of this accident and encourage them, if they do not already do so, to revise their driver scheduling practices to reduce scheduling variability that results in irregular work-rest cycles.

The Safety Board has addressed the issue of operator fatigue and the need to provide employees with fatigue awareness training in other sectors of transportation. In 1995, the Safety Board issued Safety Recommendation H-95-5, which asked the FHWA and trucking organizations to: [56]

> Develop and disseminate, in consultation with the U.S. Department of Transportation Human Factors Coordinating Committee, a training and education module to inform truckdrivers of the hazards of driving while fatigued. The module should include information about the need for an adequate amount of quality sleep, strategies for avoiding sleep loss, consideration of the behavioral

---

[52] Agent, K.R. and Pigman, J.G. "Accidents Involving Vehicles Parked on Shoulders of Limited Access Highways," *Transportation Research Record 1270.* 1990; Charles, M.T., Crank, J., and Falcone, D.N. *A Search for Evidence of the Fascination Phenomenon in Road Side Accidents.* AAA Foundation for Traffic Safety, 1990; Davis, C.C. *Accidents Involving Stopped Vehicles on Freeway Shoulders (Moth Effect Phenomenon).* Automobile Club of Southern California, 1982; and Wells, J.D. *Patrol Car Crashes: Rear End Collision Study.* Florida Highway Patrol, 1999.

[53] Safety Study Report NTSB/SS-95/01.

[54] Mitler, M., Carskadon, M., Czeisler, C. et al., "Catastrophes, Sleep, and Public Policy: Consensus Report," *Sleep 11,* 1988.

[55] *Fatigue Resource Directory.* Website: <http://olias.arc.nasa.gov/zteam/fredi/home-page.html>. Compiled in conjunction with the NASA/NTSB *Symposium Managing Fatigue in Transportation: Promoting Safety and Productivity* and managed by the DOT. Also, *Online Medical Dictionary.* Website: <http://www.graylab.ac.uk/omd/contents/F.html>.

[56] Safety Study Report NTSB/SS-95/01.

and physiological consequences of sleepiness, and an awareness that sleep can occur suddenly and without warning to all drivers regardless of their age or experience.

The FHWA subsequently worked with several different organizations to educate truckdrivers about the dangers of driving while drowsy, which resulted in the Safety Board classifying Safety Recommendation H-95-5 "Closed—Acceptable Action" in July 1998. The FHWA developed brochures and videotapes, such as "Awake at the Wheel," "Alert Driver," and "Fatigue and the Truck Driver." Although the FHWA developed its fatigue awareness brochures and videotapes with the trucking industry in mind, the information provided in them applies to the motorcoach industry as well.

According to FHWA officials, the agency has a stated goal of educating all seven million CDL holders about recognizing fatigue and about the importance of adequate rest and healthy work and lifestyle choices. In June 1999, the FHWA began a two-phase project to specifically address busdriver fatigue. The first phase, which was scheduled to be completed in December 1999, is a study of the differences between motorcoach operations and truck operations as they relate to operator fatigue. The second phase is the development of a fatigue awareness and countermeasure video for motorcoach drivers, which was scheduled to be completed and distributed in February 2000. The Safety Board is encouraged that the FHWA recognizes that fatigue is a major safety concern and applauds its efforts to educate both truckdrivers and busdrivers.

Carrier Oversight

Interstate carriers such as Greyhound, according to statistics, have consistently been a safe mode of transportation. From 1989 to 1998, a total of 54 motorcoach occupant fatalities occurred.[57] This comprised only 0.01 percent of the 419,171 highway fatalities that occurred during that time span. In 1997, motorcoaches averaged 0.04 crashes per million miles traveled, compared with 1.9 crashes for passenger cars and 2.5 crashes for large trucks.[58] Greyhound was given a satisfactory rating at its last compliance review in July 1997; its accident rate was 0.24 per 100 million miles traveled.[59] As of October 1997, the out-of-service rate for Greyhound buses was 6 percent, compared with the national average for commercial vehicles of 25.4 percent.

During the investigation of this accident, the Safety Board examined several aspects of the Greyhound safety operations, including safety incentives, training, speeding, scheduling, pre- and posttrip inspections, records and logs, and the 1-800-SAFEBUS program. Several concerns developed about the shortcomings in the oversight of the driver safety program that allow unsafe driving practices to persist or go unchecked.

---

[57] National Safety Council. *Accident Facts*. (1989-1998). Washington, DC.

[58] National Highway Traffic Safety Administration. 1998. *Traffic Safety Facts 1997*. U.S. Department of Transportation. Washington, DC.

[59] A commercial vehicle accident rate from 0.00 to 0.299 is satisfactory, 0.30 to 1.00 is conditional, and anything greater than 1.00 is unsatisfactory.

Training. According to Greyhound policy, all training provided to or attended by its employees is to be documented. The Safety Board noted several instances in which Greyhound failed to document either the content, duration, or administration of training. In 1992, the accident driver completed a required 1-day refresher course after an absence of more than 30 days. The trainer noted that the driver "could use" another refresher course in 3 to 6 months. Greyhound could not provide the Safety Board with the training manual used in a 1-day refresher course. In addition, no documentation was found that showed that the follow-up refresher course was ever administered. In 1996, a personnel entry form stated that the driver was required to take a 2-day refresher course after he had struck a parked car. As was the case previously, no documentation was found in the driver's file indicating that he had attended or successfully completed the 2-day refresher course. A random review by the Safety Board of 40 personnel and driver qualification files revealed further lack of company-required documentation.

The Safety Board concludes that Greyhound's lax procedures in compiling course material and documenting personnel training makes its safety oversight program less effective.

Safety Assessments. The Safety Board's examination of the busdriver's driving record indicated that he had three speeding violations, one each in 1989, 1992, and 1994. The 1992 and 1994 violations occurred while he was operating a bus. In addition, between 1990 and 1996, he had been involved in nine motor vehicle accidents, varying in severity, while operating a bus. In one of these accidents in 1995, he was ticketed for an unsafe lane change.

However, the busdriver's records also disclosed that between April 1988 and January 1994, he had received five Greyhound safe driving awards. These awards were issued during a period in which the driver, while operating a bus, had been involved in four accidents and had received a speeding ticket. Currently, Greyhound's safe driver program awards drivers solely for completing 6 or 12 consecutive months of driving without a preventable accident; the program does not consider traffic violations in the award process.

The Safety Board concludes that the effectiveness of the Greyhound safety oversight program is lessened by not considering traffic violations in driver safety assessments. The Safety Board believes that the UMA and the ABA should encourage their members, if they do not already do so, to include all traffic violations in their drivers' records and consider these violations during driver safety assessments. The Safety Board's safety recommendation regarding Greyhound consideration of traffic violations is discussed later in this report.

Systemwide Busdriver Speeding. Although speeding was not a factor in this accident, the Safety Board found during its investigation that busdriver speeding was prevalent throughout the Greyhound system. Safety Board investigators observed Greyhound operations at 10 terminals in different locations throughout the United States and determined that excessive speeding on the part of drivers was systemwide and not restricted to a specific operational area or geographical region. On the 40 trips that investigators observed, all 40 drivers were speeding at some time during their trips. Greyhound safety officials observed an additional 140 buses, all of which exceeded the posted speed limits. In all, 100 percent of the 180 buses observed by Safety Board investigators and Greyhound safety officials were involved in speeding. Although Greyhound buses were equipped with speed-limiting devices for the engines, the buses could exceed the governed speed on downhill grades.

The Greyhound safety oversight system relies on log book audits of hours-of-service, limited observations of drivers, and the 1-800-SAFEBUS program. But Greyhound's analysis of driver logs does not appear to be successful in detecting abnormal or excessive speed. The calculations based on the logs of 35 of the 40 drivers that the Safety Board observed speeding revealed varying and highly unlikely average speeds, such as three drivers who averaged 20 to 25 mph on a run, one driver who averaged 120 mph, and another driver who averaged 247 mph.

While busdrivers' speeding was found to be prevalent throughout the Greyhound system, the company has not employed all available means, such as monitoring drivers' violations and analyzing drivers' logs, to identify speeding and other unsafe driving practices. Therefore, the Safety Board concludes that Greyhound's current operational oversight program is inadequate to detect and correct the widespread speeding of its busdrivers. Consequently, the Safety Board believes that Greyhound should include in its drivers' assessment programs all driver traffic and logbook violations.

Use of Electronic Control Module Data. At the time of the accident, Greyhound had chosen not to activate the data pages option of the DDEC III ECM units. In the inactive condition, the data pages information was still being captured but could be accessed only by the manufacturer. According to the Greyhound senior vice president of operations, Greyhound did not perceive a need for using the data pages recording option.

The ECM data collected during routine preventative maintenance periods were extracted not to obtain driver practices information and speed history but strictly to determine that the governed speed of the buses had not been tampered with and to monitor fuel consumption.

Safety Board examination of the accident coach's ECM data, which Detroit Diesel had extracted, prompted concern about the speeds at which the accident coach had been operated over the last several months. The ECM data downloaded from the accident bus indicated that it had traveled at speeds as high as 76 mph on the day of the accident. For the previous 90 days, the data also revealed 15 instances in which the coach's speed ranged between 80 and 90 mph and 34 instances in which the speed ranged between 71 and 80 mph. This same information was readily available to Greyhound to assist the company in its driver oversight program.

According to the Greyhound vice president of operations, Greyhound plans to have older engines remanufactured and equipped with DDEC III ECM units. By spring 2000, the company expects to be operating between 1,500 and 1,700 coaches with DDEC III and IV ECM units. In November 1999, Greyhound's safety director informed the Safety Board that because of privacy issues, Greyhound has no plans to use the data pages option of the ECM units for driver oversight.

The ECM data were a powerful investigative tool for the Safety Board during this investigation. The ECM information not only supported the TransAm driver's statements, but assisted in reconstructing the TransAm and Greyhound drivers' record-of-duty status (logs) and supplied critical vehicle operational data. While a useful tool for accident investigation, its best use would be for accident prevention. Present day technology, as well as related emerging technologies, provides the Safety Board and corporate safety officials with very important fact-gathering tools. However, unless these systems are in place and their use mandated, the data will be overlooked or unavailable.

The Safety Board concludes that, by not establishing a policy to activate and use the data pages option of the ECM units, Greyhound is severely degrading its ability to oversee driver and vehicle operations safety. The Safety Board believes that Greyhound should use all current and future data monitoring and storage capabilities of ECMs, ECUs, and similar technologies to enhance vehicle and driver oversight programs by engaging the specific capabilities of each individual unit's programmed or programmable functions to collect and monitor data including, but not limited to, vehicle speed, revolutions per minute, hard-brake or sudden decelerations, and other parameters of vehicle and engine operations.

"Require devices that will automatically record specified information" is listed as one of the Safety Board's "Most Wanted" Transportation Safety Improvements.[60] The Safety Board considers adequate on-board recording devices necessary in all modes of transportation because information from them can be used to identify safety issues, develop corrective actions, and conduct more thorough, efficient accident investigations. In the past, the Safety Board has recommended that the FHWA require on-board recorders to monitor commercial drivers' hours-of-service or duty status. More recently, the Safety Board has addressed the accident investigation benefits of recording devices in recommendations urging that vehicle crash pulse data be collected.[61]

The Safety Board addressed the desirability of having crash pulse data for vehicle crashes during its 1997 Air Bag Forum.[62] On July 1, 1997, the Safety Board issued the following safety recommendation to the National Highway Traffic Safety Administration (NHTSA):

H-97-18

Develop and implement, in conjunction with the domestic and international automobile manufacturers, a plan to gather better information on crash pulses and

---

[60] Safety Recommendation H-98-26.

[61] National Transportation Safety Board. Airbag Forum NTSB/RP-97/01; 1998. *Multiple Vehicle Crossover Accident, Slinger, Wisconsin, February 12, 1997*. Highway Accident Report NTSB/HAR-98/01. Washington, D.C.; May 1999 International Symposium on Transportation Recorders; and August 1999 Hearing on Advanced Safety Technology Applications for Commercial Vehicles.

[62] NTSB/RP-97/01.

other crash parameters in actual crashes, utilizing current or augmented crash sensing and recording devices.

NHTSA responded on March 30, 1999, and indicated that it was working on this issue through its Event Data Recorder Working Group, which is composed of government and industry officials. NHTSA noted a number of activities being carried out: define event data recorder functional and performance requirements, understand present technology, develop a set of data definitions, discuss various uses of the data, and resolve legal and privacy issues. The Safety Board responded on June 17, 1999, noting the NHTSA efforts to make progress on this issue and changing the classification of Safety Recommendation H-97-18 from "Open—Unacceptable Response" to "Open—Acceptable Response."

Cockpit voice recorders and flight data recorders have been on commercial airliners for years. Since 1993, event recorders have been required on trains. Additionally, the Safety Board has for more than 20 years recommended the use of voyage event recorders for marine accident reconstruction.

The Safety Board has also made recommendations regarding recorders for highway trucking transport. In 1990,[63] the Safety Board issued the following recommendation to the FHWA:

H-90-28

Require automated/tamper-proof on-board recording devices, such as tachographs or computerized logs, to identify commercial truckdrivers who exceed hours-of-service regulations.

The Safety Board reiterated Safety Recommendation H-90-28 in its 1995 study on truckdriver fatigue,[64] explaining that the intent of the recommendation was to provide a tamper-proof mechanism that could be used to enforce the hours-of-service regulations, rather than relying on drivers' handwritten logs. In a February 1997 response, the FHWA acknowledged that on-board recording devices will eventually be an important tool for monitoring the hours-of-service of commercial motor vehicle drivers. However, the FHWA stated that its "position is that the benefits and practicality of on-board recorders must be firmly established before rulemaking ensues." In a July 1998 letter, the Safety Board responded that it was

> disappointed with the lack of positive action by the FHWA on this recommendation. While the deliberately paced research and symposium approach may yield useful information, there is no indication of aggressive research and prompt action to develop and require advanced technical solutions to address the intent of Safety Recommendation H-90-28.

As a result, the recommendation was classified "Closed—Unacceptable Action."

---

[63] National Transportation Safety Board. 1990. *Fatigue, Alcohol, Other Drugs, and Medical Factors in Fatal-to-the-Driver Heavy Truck Crashes*. Safety Study NTSB/SS-90/01. Washington, D.C.

[64] NTSB/SS-95/01.

On November 3, 1998, the FHWA again acknowledged that on-board recording devices may eventually be an important tool in monitoring commercial motor vehicle driver's hours-of-service. However, its position remains that the benefits and practicality of on-board recorders must be firmly established before rulemaking ensues. With the current state of technology, on-board recorders cannot record the duty status of the driver when the driver is not in the driving mode. The FHWA believes that it would be premature to require technology since the technology is not currently capable of all inclusive monitoring of driver fatigue. On February 25, 1999, the Safety Board noted the "lack of positive action by the FHWA on this recommendation." Should the FHWA decide to require automated tamper-proof on-board recording devices on commercial motor vehicles, the Safety Board will reevaluate the status of this recommendation. In the meantime, Safety Recommendation H-90-28 remains "Closed—Unacceptable Action."

In the Slinger, Wisconsin, accident report,[65] because the FHWA had not yet effectively acted on Safety Recommendation H-90-28, the Safety Board issued Safety Recommendation H-98-23 to the ATA, the International Brotherhood of Teamsters, and the Motor Freight Carrier Association and Safety Recommendation H-98-26 to the Independent Truckers and Drivers Association, the National Private Truck Council, and the Owner-Operators Independent Drivers Association, Inc. These recommendations are as follows:

H-98-23

Advise your members to equip their commercial vehicle fleets with automated and tamper-proof on-board recording devices, such as tachographs or computerized recorders, to identify information concerning both driver and vehicle operating characteristics.

H-98-26

Advise your members to equip their commercial vehicle fleets with automated and tamper-proof on-board recording devices, such as tachometers or computerized recorders, to identify information concerning both driver and vehicle operating characteristics.

The International Brotherhood of Teamsters, the Motor Freight Carrier Association, and the Owner-Operators Independent Drivers Association, Inc., have failed to respond to the recommendations.

The Independent Truckers and Drivers Association and the National Private Truck Council responded on August 31, 1998, and September 1, 1998, respectively, stating that they disagreed with the recommended action and would not recommend to their members that they put recording devices on their vehicles. On December 9 and 10, 1998, the Board classified Safety Recommendation H-98-26 to these addressees "Closed—Unacceptable Action."

---

[65] NTSB/HAR-98/01.

The ATA responded on September 9, 1998, that it had undertaken several steps toward implementing the recommended action and had begun the design of a simulator validation study and the development of an annual simulator. After reviewing the ATA response, the Safety Board classified Safety Recommendation H-98-23 "Open—Unacceptable Response" on January 3, 2000.

The Safety Board is convinced that in heavy commercial vehicles, significant safety benefits can be realized from tamper-proof on-board recorders that 1) continuously monitor the vehicle's operational parameters; 2) capture vehicle usage information as well as vehicle operational data, such as speed, braking, lighting, and steering; 3) are able to recognize an accident or catastrophic system failure; and 4) recapture and store predetermined time frame data before and after incident recognition. On-board recorders should have a power back-up provision or internal battery, and the unit should be placed in a crashworthy position on the vehicle. Having this operational data immediately available would enhance the accuracy of commercial vehicle accident investigations, document driver operational factors, and improve company oversight.

1-800-SAFEBUS Program. In its safety manual, Greyhound describes the 1-800-SAFEBUS program as one of its driver safety check programs. The purpose of the program is to allow the public to notify the company, using a toll-free telephone number, about driver performance, service, and driving behavior. The program is intended to make Greyhound aware of a driver's unsafe driving practices and allow the company to initiate a follow-up investigation or review of the complaints received.

Although a number of problems identified by the Safety Board, such as not recording calls and not including all complaint information in a file report, were rectified, according to Greyhound, when Fleetsafe purchased Safetynet, the Safety Board is concerned that Greyhound is not using the complaints received through the 1-800-SAFEBUS program to their full potential as a driver assessment tool. According to Greyhound, complaints are filed at a driver's home terminal but not included in that driver's personnel or qualification files, and the driver's supervisor is not required to act on a complaint. The Greyhound safety department may initiate disciplinary action for a driver who is repeatedly listed on 1-800-SAFEBUS monthly reports, presenting the possibility that a driver problem may continue for several months before action is taken. In addition, the omission of 1-800-SAFEBUS complaints from personnel files makes it more difficult for Greyhound to take a proactive stance on preventing unsafe driver practices.

When a 1-800-SAFEBUS complaint is received from an identified caller who leaves a telephone number, the Greyhound safety department is notified. However, if a complaint is received from an anonymous caller, the complaint is not processed, and the safety department is not notified; therefore, no further action is taken. Not recording all complaints increases the likelihood that unsafe driving practices will continue unchecked. Therefore, the Safety Board concludes that Greyhound's policy of disregarding anonymous calls to 1-800-SAFEBUS prevents the company from identifying patterns of unsafe driving practices by particular drivers or on particular runs and diminishes the potential safety oversight benefits of this program. Including all complaints in driver personnel files would enable Greyhound to better detect an operator problem and act to eliminate it before an accident occurs.

Receiving and following up on all calls received through the 1-800-SAFEBUS program would allow more encompassing safety oversight. Consequently, the Safety Board believes Greyhound should revise its 1-800-SAFEBUS program to ensure that all complaints are included in drivers' files and used in drivers' assessments.

Highway Factors

The Safety Board's investigation focused on the design of the emergency pull-off area and the consequences of commercial vehicles being parked in the pull-off area. A discussion of these factors, as well as of the adequacy of commercial vehicle parking spaces nationally, follows.

Use of Pull-Off Areas. Emergency pull-off areas exist along the turnpike to allow vehicles to park away from the travel lanes during an emergency. The Safety Board found, in addition to marked emergency pull-off areas, unmarked pull-off areas and picnic areas along the turnpike. This multiple-vehicle accident occurred in a marked 28-foot-wide emergency pull-off area adjacent to the westbound lanes of the turnpike. The TransAm truck struck by the Greyhound motorcoach was parked about 9 to 10 feet from the edge of the travel lane.

The Pennsylvania Turnpike guidelines follow the American Association of State Highway and Transportation Officials (AASHTO) recommendations for highway design. AASHTO recommends that roadways have a clear zone, which it defines as the total roadside border area, starting at the edge of the traveled way, available for safe use by errant vehicles. This area may consist of a shoulder, a recoverable slope, a nonrecoverable slope, and/or a clear run-out area. The desired width is dependent upon the traffic volumes and speeds and on the roadside geometry.[66] Given that the speed limit on the accident section of the turnpike is 65 mph, the average daily traffic volume in 1998 was approximately 20,000 vehicles, and the slope of shoulder adjacent to the pull-off area is 4.2 percent (1:20), the AASHTO recommended minimum clear zone would be a width of 30 feet. Therefore, the trucks that were parked there at the time of the accident were within the clear zone. Because the accident site pull-off area has a width of 28 feet, it is too small to accommodate both a 30-foot clear zone and parking for commercial or private vehicles. The turnpike has other emergency, unmarked, and picnic pull-off areas that are also unable to accommodate both a clear zone and parking for vehicles.

The 28-foot tire mark probably made by the accident motorcoach suggests that the driver had been in the process of braking shortly before impact. The Safety Board examined what might have happened had the trucks not been in the clear zone. At the calculated minimum speed of 50 mph, the stopping distance (skid distance) would have been between 167 and 208 feet. Based on this skid-to-stop distance and the available space of 230 feet to the embankment, the Safety Board determined that the motorcoach would

---

[66] *Roadside Design Guide.* American Association of State Highway and Transportation Officials. 1996.

not have collided with the embankment. However, given the same set of circumstances at a speed of 65 mph, the required skid-to-stop distance would have been between 282 and 352 feet, and the motorcoach would have collided with the embankment between 38 and 28 mph. At 70 mph, the required skid-to-stop distance would have been between 327 and 408 feet, and the motorcoach would have collided with the embankment between 46 and 38 mph.

The Safety Board has determined that the busdriver drifted off the roadway and then collided with the TransAm tractor-semitrailer parked within the 28-foot clear zone in the emergency parking pull-off area. Evidence suggests that the motorcoach probably would have struck the embankment had no vehicles been in the pull-off area; however, the impact speed would have been lower and the consequences less severe. Therefore, the Safety Board concludes that had a clear zone been available to the Greyhound driver, he may have had the opportunity to recover.

The Safety Board understands that the Commission is examining and evaluating pull-off areas and closing those that pose a risk to the motoring public. However, a postaccident survey of the turnpike by the Safety Board suggested that it was not uncommon for trucks to park close to the travel lanes. The Safety Board therefore believes that the Commission should prohibit nonemergency parking in pull-off areas within the highway clear zone. In addition, the Safety Board believes that the Commission should provide adequate rest areas for nonemergency parking to accommodate vehicles that may be displaced by the prohibition of parking in emergency pull-off areas within the highway clear zone.

Rest Areas. The drivers of the TransAm and the Oliver trucks originally parked in the emergency pull-off area because of the heavy rain. However, at the time the accident occurred, the emergency conditions that forced the drivers to pull off the roadway had passed, and both were using the pull-off as a rest area. As a result, the Safety Board explored whether the drivers' decisions may have been influenced by the insufficiency of parking at designated rest areas on the turnpike.

The lack of data on the number of rest area spaces available on the turnpike inhibited investigators from determining whether a shortfall of parking spaces existed. However, the 1996 ATA report found a shortfall of more than 28,000 truck parking spaces nationwide and of almost 2,000 commercial vehicle parking spaces in Pennsylvania. This lack of commercial vehicle parking is a national concern because it creates situations that may force fatigued drivers to stay on the road. In the 1990 Safety Board study[67] of 182 heavy truck accidents that were fatal to the driver, fatigue was a factor in 31 percent of the accidents.

The lack of adequate rest area parking spaces can also lead to overflow situations in which drivers are being compelled to park on the shoulder of rest area exit and entrance ramps. This situation is unacceptable for several reasons. First, it limits the acceleration rate of the drivers who are parked on the exit ramp shoulder, creating the possibility that

---

[67] NTSB/SS-90/01 and NTSB/SS-90/02.

their trucks' speed may be significantly lower than that of the traffic on the main roadway. Second, it creates a dangerous dilemma between high-speed vehicles decelerating into or accelerating out of the rest area and slow-moving vehicles pulling out from parking on the shoulders. Finally, the shoulders are not protected from errant vehicles. While truckdrivers may consider that this is a protected site due to the gore[68] areas that separate the ramps from the mainline, the following accident (depicted in figure 11) illustrates differently. On June 3, 1999, a westbound truck tractor-semitrailer approaching a public rest area on I-40 near Jackson, Tennessee, left the roadway, traveled 360 feet across a 63-foot-wide gore area, and struck three combination vehicles. These trucks were parked in an unauthorized area along the outside shoulder of the acceleration lane leading from the rest area onto I-40. The collision resulted in five fatalities.[69]

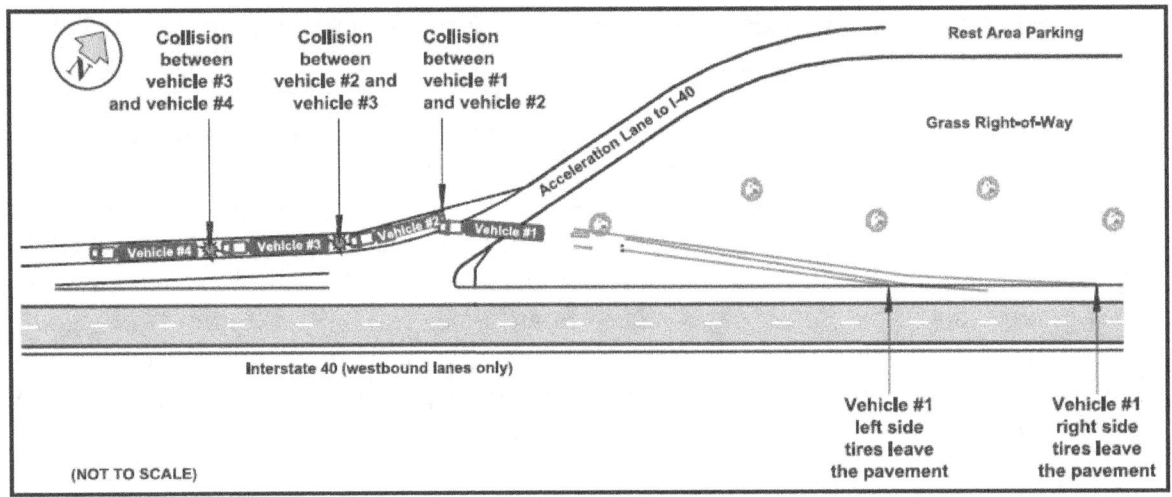

Figure 11. Diagram of truck tractor-semitrailer collision near Jackson, Tennessee.

The rest area issue has been addressed in Section 4027 of TEA 21. Section 4027 requires the DOT to perform a nationwide inventory of rest areas and other parking facilities along the national highway system and an analysis of shortages, real and projected, and to develop a plan to reduce the shortages. It stipulates that this research is to be conducted in cooperation with research organizations that represent the motor carrier industry, the travel plaza industry, and commercial motor vehicle drivers. In June 1999, OMCHS representatives met with State transportation officials to commence the process to accomplish the directive in Section 4027. The Safety Board is encouraged that a national effort has finally been initiated to alleviate the commercial vehicle parking problem and awaits the conclusions and agreements generated from the OMCHS efforts.

---

[68] The term "gore" refers to the area between a through roadway and an exit ramp and the area between a through roadway and a converging entrance ramp.

[69] National Transportation Safety Board. Docket No. Highway 99-FH-019.

Survival Aspects

Interior Lighting. One passenger said that the bus was "pitch black" after the accident. She stated that because no lights were on, the passengers had difficulty finding the emergency exits, thus slowing the evacuation. At one point, a passenger ignited a cigarette lighter to provide interior illumination, even with the smell of fuel fumes present. When the emergency responders arrived on scene, wounded passengers were trapped within the vehicle, and the interior of the bus was completely dark. Fortuitously, the first arriving emergency response vehicle had a generator to provide lighting; otherwise, the emergency responders would have had only flashlights to light the rescue operations before the arrival of a heavy-duty rescue mutual aid department. Interior emergency lighting would have helped not only the passengers in their attempt to evacuate the bus, but also the immediate emergency responders in their effort to find and treat trapped and incapacitated passengers.

Other modes of transportation, such as aviation, rail, and marine, have requirements for provision of emergency lighting during crash rescue operations. For example, in the aviation industry, carriers are required to install, and to ensure that passengers are aware of, interior emergency floor lighting, which in the event of an emergency illuminates a pathway to emergency exits. In all modes of transportation, the provision of emergency lighting decreases the likelihood of injury or death from either panic or the inability to find an available exit that may have been obvious during daylight.

The Safety Board has long believed that the capability to evacuate intercity-type buses[70] rapidly in emergencies is essential. In September 1986, as a result of its investigation of an October 1984 truck-bus head-on collision near Laredo, Texas,[71] the Safety Board asked the FHWA, in conjunction with NHTSA, to adopt standards to require emergency interior lighting for intercity-type buses that is of sufficient intensity and duration to aid occupants in identifying available exit routes and to aid rescuers in assisting injured occupants (Safety Recommendation H-86-63). After the FHWA responded on November 20, 1986, that it did not find sufficient justification to issue standards for emergency interior lighting for intercity buses, this recommendation was classified "Closed—Unacceptable Action" on March 5, 1987. Currently, no Federal standards for motorcoaches include provision of an alternate light source in the event of an accident in which the main light source has been damaged and no longer provides interior lighting.

The Safety Board concludes that the lack of Federal standards requiring motorcoaches to be equipped with reliable emergency lighting fixtures with a self-contained independent power source puts passengers in jeopardy and can hamper emergency response. Therefore, the Safety Board believes that NHTSA should revise the Federal Motor Vehicle Safety Standards (FMVSS) to require that all motorcoaches be

---

[70] Defined as for-hire buses that have a gross-vehicle-weight rating of more than 10,000 pounds and that transport more than 20 passengers.

[71] National Transportation Safety Board. 1985. *1982 Eagle Charter Coach Head-on Collision with 1983 Ford Pickup Truck, near Laredo, Texas, October 20, 1984.* Highway Field Report NTSB/HFR-85/02. Fort Worth, Texas.

equipped with emergency lighting fixtures that are outfitted with a self-contained independent power source.

Emergency Exit Signage. One of the passengers said that when evacuating the bus, everyone used the same emergency exit window to escape. He stated that he did not understand why the other windows did not automatically open when the accident occurred. He added that at first it appeared impossible to escape since, because of the darkness, no way out was apparent. Although he had years of experience riding Greyhound buses, he said he never noticed the emergency signage indicating the exit locations and the instructions on how to use them. Another passenger stated that she evacuated the bus through an exit already opened by another passenger and was the second to exit the bus because she had observed the window being opened. Therefore, the Safety Board concludes that the emergency egress of the passengers was impeded because the motorcoach lacked easily identifiable interior emergency instruction signage.

The first emergency responders who arrived on scene stated that they were unsure of how to enter the accident bus and saw no signage for entry locations or emergency exits. According to the emergency responders, without the assistance of the Greyhound busdriver who had stopped after the accident, they would not have been able to immediately gain access to the interior of the vehicle to assist the injured. When they arrived on scene they had to first set up a step ladder, which the Greyhound driver used to climb into the bus. Then he showed them how to take off the windows to gain access to the bus. When passersby and emergency responders arrive on scene to rescue trapped passengers and provide medical assistance, any impediment to rapid entry into the accident vehicle can be detrimental to timely treatment of injuries and, possibly, to passenger survival. The Safety Board concludes that, had it not been for the other Greyhound driver, who pointed out the location and demonstrated the operation of the emergency windows, the fire and rescue personnel would have lost valuable time in trying to access the bus and would not have been able to quickly provide medical assistance to the trapped passengers.

Currently, the FMVSS provide guidance only on the location of emergency signage and on what the signage should state. Furthermore, the FMVSS have no requirement that, in the event of an emergency in which normal lighting conditions do not exist, the emergency exits must be visible to the passengers. Title 49 CFR 571.217.S5.5.2 states that in buses, other than school buses, each marking shall be legible when the only source of light is the normal nighttime illumination of the bus interior. However, this requirement does not consider whether the signage is visible without the normal nighttime illumination of the interior when the vehicle has been in an accident and the main power source is no longer available. The Safety Board concludes that the current FMVSS are not comprehensive enough because the standards fail to recognize the need for interior luminescent and exterior retroreflective emergency signage in the event that interior lighting is not present during an accident or other emergency. Therefore, the Safety Board believes that NHTSA should revise the FMVSS to require the use of interior luminescent or exterior retroreflective material or both to mark all emergency exits in all motorcoaches.

Passenger Safety Briefings. In its special investigation report[72] of selected motorcoach issues, the Safety Board discussed making safety briefings available to bus passengers. Carriers have a variety of opportunities to provide passengers with emergency evacuation information. Depending on the size of the carrier or the scope of its operation, safety materials could include all or any number of the following: videos, briefings, pamphlets, or cards that are attached to seatbacks.

Safety Board investigators discussed the availability of safety briefing videos with representatives from the two major trade associations, the ABA and the UMA, and a marketing and tour brokering organization, the National Motorcoach Network (NMN). The NMN representatives said that many carriers, with the exception of Greyhound and some companies serving senior citizen groups, have motorcoaches that are equipped with television monitors that can show videotapes. The UMA, ABA, and NMN representatives said that passenger safety videos similar to those shown on aircraft are available, but are not widely used throughout the motorcoach industry.

The Safety Board has stressed the importance of passenger safety education in all modes of transportation. Federal Aviation Administration (FAA) regulations at 14 CFR Parts 121 and 135 provide minimum requirements for conveying safety information to passengers. FAA advisory circulars and air carrier operations bulletins provide general guidance to air carriers and to FAA inspectors for developing flight attendant oral safety presentations and safety cards. The guidance generally is about what information should be presented, but not how it should be presented.[73] Although the Federal Railroad Administration does not specifically include information requirements in its passenger safety regulations, Amtrak uses signs and placards, as well as briefings, to inform passengers about safety features on its trains. U.S. Coast Guard regulations require safety drills on all cruise ships embarking passengers from U.S. ports.

The Safety Board determined that emergency instructions can be crucial to a safe and expedient evacuation in the event of an accident or emergency. On February 26, 1999, the Safety Board urged the ABA and the UMA in Safety Recommendations H-99-13 and -17, respectively, to encourage their members to provide pretrip passenger safety briefings. After Safety Recommendation H-99-13 was issued, the Safety Board contacted the ABA, and no response has been received. Safety Recommendation H-99-13 is classified "Open—Await Response." Safety Recommendation H-99-17 was classified "Closed—Acceptable Action" on November 16, 1999, based on the UMA's action to make both video and script passenger briefing materials available to member companies for their use.

---

[72] National Transportation Safety Board. 1999. *Selective Motorcoach Issues.* Highway Special Investigation Report NTSB/SIR-99/01. Washington, DC.

[73] See Safety Study—*Airline Passenger Safety Education: A Review of Methods Used to Present Safety Information* (NTSB/SS-85/09).

Emergency Response

The Commission acknowledged that, without a proficient ICS, as well as procedures for control, coordination, and communication with and throughout all responding resources, the effectiveness of emergency response is reduced. One of the turnpike ICS goals is to achieve better communication and coordination at the scene among fire and rescue, ambulance service, PSP, turnpike maintenance personnel, and other agencies. The ICS for this accident included numerous mutual aid agencies contracted by the Commission. Although the emergency response was adequate, the Safety Board identified several areas, such as communications equipment, initial dispatch of appropriate rescue equipment, and disaster response and management, that need improvement.

Communications Equipment. According to the turnpike *Incident Management Program Manual*, when an incident occurs on the turnpike, the maintenance department is responsible for setting up a mobile command post, which is used to coordinate organization and communications. Additionally, standard first responder vans are to be equipped with cellular phones, CB radios, turnpike repeaters, and portable radios; the customized emergency response vehicles are to provide enhanced communication at the scene. The Commission was to provide radios to contracted fire services and EMS responders that did not have radios compatible with the turnpike's communication system to ensure that when an incident occurred, all responding State police, turnpike units, and emergency services would be capable of communicating with each other during their response.

The Metal Township fire chief, who acted as the fire and rescue IC, stated that one problem he encountered on scene was that the medical channel and fire radio channels used different frequencies and the other responding counties also had a different radio frequency; as a result, three or four different radios were needed to communicate. The IC said that he did not have the necessary radios available and that a communication lapse occurred that left him unable to communicate with everyone who was on scene.

One problem due to the lack of communication occurred when, during triage, the Fulton County Medical Center could not handle any more patients, and the medics had to send the patients to Chambersburg Hospital. The IC said that he was unaware of this situation because the information was broadcast only on the medical channel and he had a low band channel for the fire company activities; therefore, the IC was dispatching conflicting instructions to emergency responders. He recalled that the medical response became chaotic and disorganized for a period of time, although overall, it did not have a negative effect on the medical assistance provided to the injured.

The turnpike's *Incident Management Manual* goal in using the ICS -- to achieve better communication and coordination at the scene among all responders -- was not achieved during the emergency response to the Burnt Cabins accident. Because the IC for fire and rescue did not have the appropriate radios, he could not communicate with all the responding agencies at the scene; as a result, the emergency response was disorganized and, at times, chaotic. The Safety Board, therefore, concludes that, during emergency response activities for the Burnt Cabins accident, the communications were not adequate to appropriately handle a mass casualty event and resulted in less than optimal emergency response.

Initial Dispatch of Appropriate Emergency Equipment. Under the box card assignment set up for turnpike accidents, a prearranged number of units are dispatched to a specific accident, a prearranged number for each situation. In this accident, the box card assignment provided for a dispatch of only four ambulances and one rescue engine. When the IC arrived on scene and assessed the situation, he found that he did not have the resources needed to deal with the accident. He then requested additional resources and equipment, including multiple ambulances and helicopters.

The fire chief and deputy fire chief of West End Fire and Rescue concurred with the IC about the dispatching of emergency equipment to the accident. They stated that, when the call was received, the situation was initially relayed as involving a bus and tractor-semitrailer. The West End department, being the closest heavy-duty response unit, should have been immediately dispatched, especially since it has the same dispatcher as Metal Township, the initial responding department. According to the West End fire chief and deputy fire chief, being dispatched initially would have saved approximately 15 minutes in arrival time, which can be vital in emergency response to an accident. Instead, their department was dispatched only after the IC arrived on scene and called for their aid.

In Franklin County where West End normally operates, its box card assignments for mass casualties always include at least two heavy-duty squads, two full engine companies, and four basic life support ambulances, as well as one or two medic units and a helicopter on standby. The fire chief and deputy fire chief said that based on the dispatch description of the accident, additional mutual aid units should have been called immediately and sent to a staging area away from the accident scene. Depending on what was happening on scene, the resources could have been dispatched without delay upon request.

The Safety Board concludes that, although not detrimental to the emergency response efforts for the accident victims, the lack of an initial dispatch of appropriate emergency rescue equipment resulted in a less expedient and more disorganized response.

Disaster Preparedness and Emergency Response Management. The turnpike *Incident Command System Manual*, available to the PSP Troop T and the contracted fire and EMS responders, featured an accident scenario in which a Greyhound bus ran off the road and down an embankment, resulting in fatal, serious, and minor injuries. The manual discussed potential problems that might be encountered and listed emergency response units and apparatus that might be required. However, the Commission did not hold any mutual aid disaster drills to provide hands-on training on any of the scenarios presented in the manual.

According to the Commission, its subcommittees for emergency services are responsible for conducting annual informational meetings with the contracted service departments. These meetings are designed so that the PSP and turnpike personnel can discuss accident and safety procedures and any operational or protocol problems with the emergency service groups. According to the *Incident Management Program Book*, these meetings have proven invaluable as a source for improving overall communications and on-scene management and have enhanced the response to turnpike incidents. However, the Metal Township fire chief, who acted as the fire and rescue IC for the accident, told Safety Board investigators that these annual group meetings were not obligatory and, therefore, he had never attended. He also said that Franklin County had, however, performed countywide disaster drills and held one a few months before this accident occurred.

In addition, the IC remarked that he had concerns about how the emergency response was conducted and believed that it could have been improved, especially in the area of emergency medical services. He recalled that even though the Metal Township EMT captain was tracking the ambulances and the patients being transported, the IC was not aware that one medical center could not receive any more of the injured and that they had to be transported to another hospital. He said that the situation was "chaotic" because Metal Township had never before dealt with an accident of this magnitude. Other emergency responders agreed; one paramedic recalled that the accident scene was "pretty much chaos" and everyone mostly did what they wanted. The IC also stated that he had not had bus rescue training before the accident occurred and that emergency responders should have training on commercial buses. Other emergency responders interviewed by the Safety Board after the accident stated that they believed having operational drills would be beneficial in the event of another mass casualty.

The Safety Board has long been a proponent of emergency response plans that specifically highlight multicasualty accidents involving numerous mutual aid agencies from varying jurisdictions. The disaster plan procedures should address, at a minimum, key emergency response departments, equipment, management personnel, and communication. Although the turnpike's manual included such information, turnpike officials had not tested the adequacy of the disaster plans or the ability of contracted emergency responders to work together to carry out their assigned functions. The Safety Board concludes that because the Commission did not provide disaster drills for its contracted emergency response personnel, the Burnt Cabins emergency response was marked by communication equipment problems, delays in dispatching the appropriate heavy rescue equipment, and a lack of coordination in providing emergency medical services. Therefore, the Safety Board believes the Commission should periodically conduct disaster drills in mass casualty transportation accidents, such as the bus accident near Burnt Cabins, with contracted emergency response departments on the turnpike to assess its emergency management plan, to reinforce and evaluate emergency training, and to test communication among the responding agencies.

Conclusions

Findings

1. Neither the existing highway pavement conditions, the mechanical condition of the bus, nor the weather contributed to the accident. The busdriver did not appear to be speeding, nor was he impaired by alcohol or illicit drugs.

2. The evidence cannot establish that the busdriver was impaired or incapacitated by a cardiac condition prior to the accident.

3. The busdriver ingested an over-the-counter multisymptom cold and allergy medication at some time either shortly before or during his scheduled route. The sedating antihistamine in this medication contributed to making the busdriver sleepy and reducing his alertness.

4. Because of the scheduled irregular work-rest cycle and possible sleeping difficulties, the busdriver may have developed a sleep debt over the 4 days of his shift, which was exacerbated by a reduced alertness corresponding to his body's circadian rhythm. The combined result of these factors may have contributed to the busdriver's sleepiness and reduced alertness, causing him to drift off the roadway and collide with the tractor-semitrailer parked in the adjacent emergency parking area.

5. Greyhound's lax procedures in compiling course material and documenting personnel training makes its safety oversight program less effective.

6. The effectiveness of the Greyhound safety oversight program is lessened by not considering traffic violations in driver safety assessments.

7. Greyhound's current operational oversight program is inadequate to detect and correct the widespread speeding of its busdrivers.

8. By not establishing a policy to activate and use the data pages option of the electronic control module units, Greyhound is severely degrading its ability to oversee driver and vehicle operations safety.

9. Greyhound's policy of disregarding anonymous calls to 1-800-SAFEBUS prevents the company from identifying patterns of unsafe driving practices by particular drivers or on particular runs and diminishes the potential safety oversight benefits of this program. Including all complaints in driver personnel files would enable Greyhound to better detect an operator problem and act to eliminate it before an accident occurs.

10. Had a clear zone been available to the Greyhound driver, he may have had the opportunity to recover.

11. The lack of Federal standards requiring motorcoaches to be equipped with reliable emergency lighting fixtures with a self-contained independent power source puts passengers in jeopardy and can hamper emergency response.

12. The emergency egress of the passengers was impeded because the motorcoach lacked easily identifiable interior emergency instruction signage.

13. Had it not been for the other Greyhound driver, who pointed out the location and demonstrated the operation of the emergency windows, the fire and rescue personnel would have lost valuable time in trying to access the bus and would not have been able to quickly provide medical assistance to the trapped passengers.

14. The current Federal Motor Vehicle Safety Standards are not comprehensive enough because the standards fail to recognize the need for interior luminescent and exterior retroreflective emergency signage in the event that interior lighting is not present during an accident or other emergency.

15. During emergency response activities for the Burnt Cabins accident, the communications were not adequate to appropriately handle a mass casualty event and resulted in less than optimal emergency response.

16. Although not detrimental to the emergency response efforts for the accident victims, the lack of an initial dispatch of appropriate emergency rescue equipment resulted in a less expedient and more disorganized response.

17. Because the Pennsylvania Turnpike Commission did not provide disaster drills for its contracted emergency response personnel, the Burnt Cabins emergency response was marked by communication equipment problems, delays in dispatching the appropriate heavy rescue equipment, and a lack of coordination in providing emergency medical services.

Probable Cause

The National Transportation Safety Board determines that the probable cause of this accident was the busdriver's reduced alertness resulting from ingesting a sedating antihistamine and from his fatigued condition resulting from Greyhound Lines, Inc., scheduling irregular work-rest periods. Contributing to the severity of the accident was the Pennsylvania Turnpike Commission's practice of routinely permitting nonemergency parking in pull-off areas within the highway clear zone.

Recommendations

As a result of its investigation, the National Transportation Safety Board makes the following recommendations:

To the National Highway Traffic Safety Administration:

Revise the Federal Motor Vehicle Safety Standards to require that all motorcoaches be equipped with emergency lighting fixtures that are outfitted with a self-contained independent power source. (H-00-01)

Revise the Federal Motor Vehicle Safety Standards to require the use of interior luminescent or exterior retroreflective material or both to mark all emergency exits in all motorcoaches. (H-00-02)

To the Pennsylvania Turnpike Commission:

Prohibit nonemergency parking in pull-off areas within the highway clear zone. (H-00-03)

Provide adequate rest areas for nonemergency parking to accommodate vehicles that may be displaced by the prohibition of parking in emergency pull-off areas within the highway clear zone. (H-00-04)

Periodically conduct disaster drills in mass casualty transportation accidents, such as the bus accident near Burnt Cabins, with contracted emergency response departments on the Pennsylvania Turnpike to assess its emergency management plan, to reinforce and evaluate emergency training, and to test communication among the responding agencies. (H-00-05)

To Greyhound Lines, Inc.:

Revise your driver scheduling practices to reduce scheduling variability that results in irregular work-rest cycles. (H-00-06)

Include in your drivers' assessment programs all driver traffic and logbook violations. (H-00-07)

Use all current and future data monitoring and storage capabilities of electronic control modules, electronic control units, and similar technologies to enhance vehicle and driver oversight programs by engaging the specific capabilities of each individual unit's programmed or programmable functions to collect and monitor data including, but not limited to, vehicle speed, revolutions-per-minute, hard-brake or sudden decelerations, and other parameters of vehicle and engine operations. (H-00-08)

Revise your 1-800-SAFEBUS program to ensure that all complaints are included in drivers' files and used in drivers' assessments. (H-00-09)

To the United Motorcoach Association:

Advise your members of the facts and circumstances of this accident and encourage them, if they do not already do so, to 1) revise their driver scheduling practices to reduce scheduling variability that results in irregular work-rest cycles and to 2) include all traffic violations in their drivers' records and consider these violations during driver safety assessments. (H-00-10)

To the American Bus Association:

Advise your members of the facts and circumstances of this accident and encourage them, if they do not already do so, to 1) revise their driver scheduling practices to reduce scheduling variability that results in irregular work-rest cycles and to 2) include all traffic violations in their drivers' records and consider these violations during driver safety assessments. (H-00-11)

BY THE NATIONAL TRANSPORTATION SAFETY BOARD

JAMES E. HALL
Chairman

JOHN A. HAMMERSCHMIDT
Member

JOHN J. GOGLIA
Member

GEORGE W. BLACK, JR.
Member

Adopted: January 5, 2000

Appendix A

Investigation

The National Transportation Safety Board was notified of the Burnt Cabins, Pennsylvania, accident about 10:30 a.m. on June 20, 1998. An investigative team was dispatched with members from the Washington, D.C.; Atlanta, Georgia; and Parsippany, New Jersey, offices. Groups were established to investigate the human performance aspects; the highway, vehicle, and survival factors; and the motor carrier operations.

Participating in the investigation were representatives of the Federal Highway Administration; the Pennsylvania Turnpike Commission; the Pennsylvania State Police; Greyhound Lines, Inc.; TransAm Trucking Incorporated; and motor coach associations.

No public hearing was held; no depositions were taken.

Appendix B

Other Vehicles

TransAm Trucking Incorporated Vehicle And Occupants

TransAm Incorporated

TransAm Trucking Incorporated owned and operated the tractor-semitrailer combination. The company, with offices in Olathe, Kansas, and Kansas City, Missouri, has 515 power units and employs 600 drivers. It is registered with the Federal Highway Administration (FHWA) as an interstate common carrier of general freight, meat, foods, beverages, and hazardous materials and has been assigned U.S. Department of Transportation (DOT) identification number 315503.

TransAm Tractor-Semitrailer

The combination vehicle three-axle 1998 Freightliner tractor, of conventional design with a sleeper berth, and the 1991 53-foot utility semitrailer refrigerated cargo van with its cargo weighed 52,300 pounds.

The tractor was equipped with a Detroit Diesel Series 60, 12.7 liter, electronically controlled diesel engine, which was outfitted with a Detroit Diesel electronic controls model III electronic controls module (ECM),[1] governed at 72 mph. At the time of inspection, the optional data pages recording capability of the ECM was enabled. After National Transportation Safety Board investigators removed the ECM, Detroit Diesel technicians extracted the data from the ECM, which they provided to the Safety Board. According to that information, the TransAm tractor had been motionless and idling on the day of the accident from about 12:30 to 4:00 a.m.,[2] at which time the ECM data indicated the engine was no longer idling.

TransAm Tractor-Semitrailer Damage

Damage was observed in the area of the sleeper compartment of the cab. The rear bulkhead of the tractor cab was deformed outward about 8 inches. No additional damage was noted to the tractor.

Both of the trailer rear doors had been removed from the trailer before inspection. The doors had been equipped with diamond grade, prismatic red and white adhesive, retroreflective conspicuity sheeting.

---

[1] A semiconductor unit for controlling ignition timing and other parameters in an engine management system.

[2] Times are approximations based on the ECM engine usage profile report.

The trailer sustained intrusion damage to and upward deformation of its rear section. The trailer frame rails had been bilaterally displaced upward. Frame rail damage was measured in 1-foot increments starting from the rear axle locking pin in the 25th aligning hole from the rear of the trailer. The last measurement represented the maximum observed deformation. The left side of the trailer exhibited 1.75 feet of outward bowing, measured at the outermost point. Maximum outward deformation along the right side of the trailer at the rear measured about 2 feet. The rear-end cap framing of the trailer was deformed outward approximately 1 foot on the left side and 0.75 foot on the right side; the bottom was deformed upward about 1 foot. The lower right and left rears of the trailer were displaced rearward approximately 2 and 6 feet, respectively. The interior flooring was displaced upward.

TransAm Tractor-Semitrailer Tests

The Safety Board's materials laboratory conducted a forensic examination of four taillight and two side marker light assemblies that were removed from the trailer. These assemblies were examined for the presence of hot stretch, and the examination revealed that the filaments in several of the bulbs did exhibit evidence of stretching.

TransAm Truck Occupants

Both occupants of the TransAm truck were in the sleeper berth at the time of the accident. The passenger sustained serious injuries involving multiple rib fractures, pulmonary contusion, and head abrasions. She said that she was thrown forward from the sleeper and landed in the cab and the truckdriver landed on top of her. The truckdriver received minor injuries involving multiple contusions, lacerations, abrasions, and sprains. He stated that he was thrown from the sleeper onto the floor of the cab.

A pretreatment blood screen was conducted on one of them at the hospital emergency room; the report was negative for drugs or alcohol. A postaccident drug test was conducted on the other occupant; these test results were also negative for alcohol and drugs. (Because the vehicle was parked at the time of the accident, the drug testing of the occupants was not required by Federal regulations.)

Oliver Trucking Incorporated Vehicle And Occupant

Oliver Trucking Incorporated

Oliver Trucking Incorporated, located in Indianapolis, Indiana, has 223 power units and employs 383 drivers. It is registered with the FHWA as a common carrier of general freight and has been assigned DOT identification number 164074.

Oliver Tractor-Semitrailer

The 1995 Kenworth model T-600 tractor, of conventional design with a sleeper berth, was leased from Penske Truck Leasing, Incorporated; the 1988 Trailmobile, semitrailer was owned and operated by Oliver Trucking Incorporated.

Oliver Tractor-Semitrailer Damage

The trailer sustained contact damage to its left side where two horizontal creases were observed. The first crease was approximately 33 inches from the bottom of the trailer and traveled from the rear about 207 inches; the second was approximately 50 inches from the bottom of the trailer and traveled from the rear about 199 inches. A 24-inch longitudinal tear to the outer skin of the semitrailer, which began approximately 125 inches from the rear, was observed along the second crease.

Oliver Truck Occupant

The occupant of the Oliver truck, who was in the sleeper berth of his cab at the time of the accident, was uninjured. No postaccident drug test was conducted on the occupant nor was it required.

Appendix C

Injury Table

INJURIES	DRIVER	BUS PASSENGERS	OTHER[a]	TOTAL
AIS 9 : UNKNOWN	0	0	0	0
AIS 6 : UNSURVIVABLE	1	1	0	2
AIS 5 : CRITICAL	0	1	0	1
AIS 4 : SEVERE	0	3	0	3
AIS 3 : SERIOUS	0	2	1	3
AIS 2 : MODERATE	0	1	0	1
AIS 1 : MINOR	0	14	1	15
AIS 0 : NONE	0	0	0	0
TOTAL[b]	1	22	2	25

a TransAm truckdr ver and codr ver
b The O ver truckdr ver was un njured not transported to a hosp ta and therefore not nc uded n the count

Injury table based on the Abbreviated Injury Scale[1] of the Association for the Advancement of Automotive Medicine.

---

[1] Abbreviated Injury Scale refers to the abbreviated injury scale (revised 1990) of the American Association for the Advancement of Automotive Medicine.

Appendix D

Federal Motor Carrier Safety Ratings Procedures

The Motor Carrier Safety Act of 1984 directed the U.S. Secretary of Transportation to establish a procedure to determine the safety fitness of owners and operators of commercial motor vehicles operating in interstate or foreign commerce. Subsequently, the FHWA promulgated a set of safety fitness standards and established a methodology for determining whether a carrier has adequate safety management controls to ensure acceptable compliance with the safety requirements. The original methodology was modified as a result of the Motor Carrier Safety Act of 1990 and a 1997 rulemaking.

Six factors (see table 1) form the basis for a carrier's safety rating, that is, the degree to which a carrier is in compliance with the Federal Motor Carrier Safety Regulations (FMCSR) and therefore meets the safety fitness standard.

Table 1. Motor carrier safety rating factors.

Factor*	Applicable FMCSR
Factor 1 - General	Parts 387 and 390
Factor 2 - Driver	Parts 382, 383, and 391
Factor 3 - Operational	Parts 392 and 395
Factor 4 - Vehicle	Parts 393 and 396
Factor 5 - Hazardous Materials	Parts 397, 171, 177, and 180
Factor 6 - Accident Factor	Recordable Preventable Rate
*A factors are g ven equa we ght	

Each factor is rated satisfactory, conditional, or unsatisfactory. A satisfactory factor rating means the carrier has not violated any acute or critical regulations. A conditional factor rating means the carrier has violated one acute regulation or has a pattern of noncompliance with critical regulations. An unsatisfactory factor rating means the carrier has violated two or more acute regulations or has patterns of noncompliance with two or more critical regulations. The accident factor is based on the carrier's size and number of accidents.

Acute violations are FMCSR or Hazardous Materials Regulation violations demanding immediate corrective action regardless of the overall safety posture of the motor carrier. For example, requiring or permitting the operation of a vehicle declared out of service before repairs are made (49 CFR 396.9[c][2]) is an acute violation.

Critical violations are regulatory violations that indicate breakdowns in a carrier's management controls. For instance, requiring or permitting a driver to drive after having been on duty for 15 hours (49 CFR 395.3[a][2]) is a critical violation.

The ratings for the first five factors and the accident rate for the 12 months before the review are then entered into a rating table, which is used to establish the motor carrier's safety rating (see table 2). Each of the six factors is given equal weight.

Table 2. Motor carrier safety rating table.

Factor Ratings		Safety Rating
Number of Unsatisfactory Ratings	Number of Conditional Ratings	Resultant Safety Rating
0	2 or fewer	Satisfactory
0	more than 2	Conditional
1	2 or fewer	Conditional
1	more than 2	Unsatisfactory
2 or more	0	Unsatisfactory